PERFECT PICKLES
CHUTNEYS & RELISHES

PERFECT PICKLES
CHUTNEYS & RELISHES

AN ESSENTIAL PRACTICAL GUIDE TO MAKING DELICIOUS PRESERVES AT HOME,
WITH MORE THAN 70 STEP-BY-STEP RECIPES AND 300 SUPERB PHOTOGRAPHS

CATHERINE ATKINSON

southwater

This edition is published by Southwater,
an imprint of Anness Publishing Ltd, Hermes House, 88–89 Blackfriars Road, London SE1 8HA;
tel. 020 7401 2077; fax 020 7633 9499

www.southwaterbooks.com; www.annesspublishing.com

If you like the images in this book and would like to investigate using them for publishing, promotions or
advertising, please visit our website www.practicalpictures.com for more information.

UK agent: The Manning Partnership Ltd; tel. 01225 478444; fax 01225 478440; sales@manning-partnership.co.uk
UK distributor: Grantham Book Services Ltd; tel. 01476 541080; fax 01476 541061; orders@gbs.tbs-ltd.co.uk
North American agent/distributor: National Book Network; tel. 301 459 3366; fax 301 429 5746; www.nbnbooks.com
Australian agent/distributor: Pan Macmillan Australia; tel. 1300 135 113; fax 1300 135 103; customer.service@macmillan.com.au
New Zealand agent/distributor: David Bateman Ltd; tel. (09) 415 7664; fax (09) 415 8892

Publisher: Joanna Lorenz
Managing Editor: Linda Fraser
Project Editors: Susannah Blake, Lucy Doncaster and Jennifer Mussett
Production Controller: Claire Rae
Photographer: Craig Robertson
Home Economist: Sarah O'Brien
Stylist: Helen Trent

ETHICAL TRADING POLICY
Because of our ongoing ecological investment programme, you, as our customer, can have the pleasure and reassurance of
knowing that a tree is being cultivated on your behalf to naturally replace the materials used to make the book you are holding.
For further information about this scheme, go to www.annesspublishing.com/trees

© Anness Publishing Ltd 2005, 2008

Previously published as part of a larger volume, *Preserves*

NOTES
Bracketed terms are intended for American readers. Medium (US large) eggs are used unless otherwise stated.
For all recipes, quantities are given in both metric and imperial measures and, where appropriate, measures are also given in
standard cups and spoons. Follow one set, but not a mixture, because they are not interchangeable.
Standard spoon and cup measures are level.
1 tsp = 5ml, 1 tbsp = 15ml, 1 cup = 250ml/8fl oz
Australian standard tablespoons are 20ml. Australian readers should use 3 tsp in place of 1 tbsp for measuring small quantities.
This book has been written with the reader's safety in mind, and the advice, information and instructions are intended to be clear and safe
to follow. However, cooking with boiling hot mixtures can be dangerous and there is a risk of burns if sufficient care is not taken. Neither the
author nor the publisher can accept any legal responsibility or liability for any errors or omissions made, or for accidents in the kitchen.

contents

INTRODUCTION

Preserving seasonal fruits and vegetables as pickles, savoury jellies, chutneys and relishes is one of the oldest of culinary arts. Once essential for basic survival, preserving is nowadays more often employed as a tasty and efficient method of storing seasonal vegetables or fruits. It can be done in two ways: by heat sterilization, which destroys enzymes and bacteria, or by creating an environment where contaminants are unable to thrive – by drying, salting, or adding sugar, vinegar or alcohol.

AN AGE-OLD TECHNIQUE

Preserving was one of the earliest skills acquired by man, and it was essential for survival during the cold, dark winter months when fresh food was scarce. Sun and wind were the first natural agents to be used: fruits and vegetables laid out in the hot sun or hung in the wind to dry were found to last longer than fresh produce and were lighter and easier to carry. In colder, damp climates, smoke and fire were used to hasten the drying process.

It wasn't long before early man found that salt was a powerful dehydrator, far more consistent and reliable than the natural elements of sun and wind. Salt soon became a highly prized commodity – so much so that wars were fought over it. In fact, sometimes the salt was more valuable than the food it preserved, hence the saying that something is not worth its salt. Using salt to preserve foods made long-distance travel more possible because produce that had previously been perishable could be taken on board ships for journeys that lasted months and sometimes even years. New settlements were built where it was now feasible for people to both grow and store food.

The preservative properties of vinegar and alcohol were discovered around the same time as those of salt, and people also realized that food could be flavoured at the same time that it was being preserved. Vinegar, which creates an acid environment that contaminants cannot live in, was used throughout the world. Malt vinegars were common in countries where beer was brewed, wine vinegar where vines were grown and rice vinegar became popular in the Far East.

Surprisingly the use of sugar as a preservative wasn't discovered until many centuries later. Cane sugar, brought to Europe by Arab merchants in the 12th century, remained a scarce luxury in the Western world for 400 years. It wasn't until the 16th century, when it was introduced to Europe from the West Indies, that sugar became a sought-after ingredient. Soon the demand for it became so great that it encouraged the rise of colonialism and the slave trade. In the 18th century, beetroot (beet), which had always been enjoyed as a vegetable, began to be cultivated specifically for its sugar content. Eventually sugar became plentiful and cheap, and the liking for sweet preserves started to grow.

It was during the 19th century that preserving really came into its own and was considered to be a skilled craft. Many of the recipes we use today are based on those that first appeared in cookbooks during that era. Housewives took pride in filling capacious larders (pantries) with bottles and jars of

Left: Rich, fruity chutneys were first made in India and became popular in Britain in the 19th century.

Above: Bottling vegetables in vinegar both preserves and flavours the food, and is a technique that is used all over the world.

pickles, relishes and chutneys made from fruit and vegetables during the summer and autumn while they were plentiful. These were then enjoyed during the lean winter months to supplement their diet, which consisted mainly of salted meats and root vegetables.

In the 20th century, preserving became less fashionable. Many homes had less storage space and, as the range and use of commercially prepared pickles and relishes increased, huge stocks of home-made preserves were no longer either needed or desirable. Imported produce meant that many fruits and vegetables were available all year round – summer vegetables could be bought in the winter months and citrus fruits never disappeared from grocers' shelves. By the middle of the century, refrigerators could be found in most homes, followed by freezers in the 1960s and '70s. During those decades freezing became the preferred way of preserving fruit and vegetables and the old-fashioned techniques became less popular and were often forgotten.

PICKLE-MAKING TODAY

Nowadays though, the art of pickling and preserving is coming back into its own, not because food needs to be processed to make it keep for long periods but for reasons of quality and variety. Improved travel and communication have increased knowledge of preserves from around the world and more unusual varieties of fruit, vegetables and flavouring ingredients are now readily available. Many people prefer to make their own preserves instead of buying mass-produced products with artificial flavourings and colourings. The satisfaction that comes from being able to create a unique product is also being rediscovered.

This book contains a comprehensive and detailed reference section showing how to make pickles, chutneys, relishes and other savoury preserves. All the main techniques are shown, including pickling and chutney- and relish-making. There is also a fabulous full-colour guide to the ingredients used for pickling and preserving – from seasonal fruits and vegetables to flavourings and preservatives.

The stunning recipe collection includes a whole host of traditional and contemporary ideas that will prove to be an inspiration and pleasure to both the novice and the experienced pickle-maker.

Below: Nowadays chutneys and pickles are made with a range of exotic ingredients, such as rhubarb and tangerine.

FRUIT

Most of the many varieties of fruit can be used to form the basis of or add flavour to pickles, chutneys, savoury jellies and relishes.

ORCHARD FRUITS

Apples and pears, which are available all year round, are the most common members of this family of fruits. Other, more unusual, orchard fruits used in preserves include quinces.

There are many varieties of apples, although choice in the shops is usually limited to just a few. Among the most popular eating apples are Gala, Russet, Granny Smith, Braeburn, Golden Delicious and Cox's Orange Pippin. Well-flavoured eating apples may also be used in

chutneys and relishes when retaining the texture of the fruit is desirable. Cooking apples are more frequently used in jellies and give a good pulpy texture to chutneys. **Apples** are high in pectin and, on their own, produce rather bland, colourless preserves. They are therefore often combined with fruits with a good flavour and low pectin content to produce a savoury jelly with a better set.

Most of the pectin in apples is found in the skin and seeds so apple peelings and cores are often used to make a pectin stock. This is then stirred into other savoury fruit jellies to improve their set, without affecting their flavour. **Pears** are low in pectin, so are less frequently used in savoury jellies. Their sweet, mild flavour and tender texture makes them popular for chutney-making and they are superb pickled in raspberry vinegar. Pears are divided into eating and cooking varieties, although some eating pears are also suitable for cooking. The British Conference and the American Bosc are particularly good for preserving.

Quinces are golden yellow and can be the size and shape of a small squat pear or a small apple, or as large as big pears, depending on the variety. The flesh is hard, granular and sour when eaten raw, but with cooking it becomes smooth and tender, with a delicate soft pink colour and a sherbet-like aromatic

Left: Apples are used in almost every type of preserve – from savoury jellies to spicy relishes.

Above: Pears work well bottled in spiced vinegars and make a tasty addition to sweet-and-sour chutneys.

flavour. Quinces are rich in pectin and they can be made into savoury jellies; these may be a rich gold or a deep pink colour depending on the variety.

STONE FRUITS

These are all fruits of the *Prunus* genus, recognized by their single central woody stone (pit), soft flesh and thin skin. They are well-suited to savoury jelly-making and can also be used whole or halved in bottled preserves. They come in a wide variety of colours, textures and flavours, from pale orange apricots and yellow-skinned plums, to sweet red cherries, and they can be made into a whole range of preserves. Plums are available all year round, and although cherries, apricots, peaches and nectarines are sometimes available at other times of the year, they are at their peak in summer and early autumn.

Plums range in colour from pale gold through red and crimson to deep purple. When buying, choose firm, unwrinkled fruit, which still have a slight bloom. They will keep for several days at room temperature, but will continue to ripen. Once they are almost ripe, they can be stored in the refrigerator for a few more days. Use them when just-ripe to make richly flavoured preserves.

Mirabelle plums are a French speciality, grown particularly around Alsace. They are small, round, red-flushed yellow plums with a powerful sweet scent. **Greengages** are small, green, fragrant plums, which are primarily dessert fruits, but which are excellent bottled.

Cherries make wonderful savoury jellies and relishes. There are two varieties: sweet cherries, which may be black (actually deep red) or white (usually yellow), and sour cherries, of which the best-known are Morellos. When buying, the cherry's stem is a good indicator of freshness – it should be green

Below: Smooth-skinned nectarines make a flavourful addition to chutneys and relishes.

Right: Sweet black cherries can be made into the most delicious, richly flavoured relishes.

and flexible not brown and brittle. Cherries are low in pectin, so must either be combined with apples or other pectin-rich fruit, or commercial or home-made pectin stock needs to be added when making savoury jellies. Both sweet and sour cherries are excellent pickled or bottled.

Peaches have downy skins and a good peach will be richly coloured and heavy. The most common types have yellow or pink flesh. The white-fleshed and pale-skinned variety is the sweetest of all.

Nectarines are similar to peaches but they have smooth and shiny skins and a slightly sharper taste – like a cross between a peach and a plum. They are good pickled or bottled, and are also excellent made into fruity chutneys. Peaches and nectarines should be skinned when making chutneys.

Apricots, with their slightly sweet-and-sour flavour, soft texture and downy skins, are delicious eaten raw. Apricots and almonds are a very popular combination and split almonds can be added to special chutneys for extra flavour and texture. When choosing apricots, pick those with the strongest colour for the sweetest flavour.

SOFT FRUITS AND BERRIES

These delicate summer fruits can be made into wonderful relishes and savoury jellies. **Raspberries** are crimson, yellow or white and have a delicious, delicate flavour. **Blackberries** are a wild fruit, native to Europe and the United States. They contain sufficient pectin to make intensely flavoured jellies, and go extremely well with apples. **Cranberries** are a member of the blueberry family. These small, hard, shiny, deep-red berries are too sour to eat raw but can be transformed into bright red jellies and rich sauces, which are traditionally served with turkey. **Gooseberries** are too sour to eat raw, but can be made into savoury jellies and chutneys. They are rich in pectin, especially when slightly unripe. **Black-, red- and white-currants** have a sharp flavour and are picked in bunches on stems. High in both pectin and acid, currants need little cooking and are often made into savoury jellies. Remove currants from the stalk by running the prongs of a fork gently down the stalk.

CITRUS FRUITS

With their aromatic acidity, citrus fruits are often added to other preserves because of their wonderful flavours and also as they have a high pectin and acid content and can help achieve a good set. Their pungency and sharpness not only adds flavour but also offsets sweetness.

Lemons are indispensable in the preserving kitchen. They add acid and pectin to savoury jellies made from low-pectin fruit such as pears and peaches, which are difficult to set. Adding lemon juice to savoury jellies also gives them a sparkling appearance. A dash of lemon juice added to preserves made from soft fruit such as blackberries and exotic fruits such as papayas helps bring out their flavour. A few spoonfuls of lemon juice added to cold water makes an acidulated dip that will prevent cut fruit such as pears and apples from discolouring. Small, thin-skinned lemons are juicier, so are perfect for making preserves.

     Limes are small green fruits which

Above: Sharp, zesty lemons are widely used in savoury preserves.

flourish in near-tropical conditions. They have a distinctive, tangy flavour and are one of the most sour citrus fruits. A squeeze of lime juice can be added to savoury jellies, relishes and chutneys instead of lemon juice to enhance the flavour of the fruit and to improve the set. They go particularly well with tropical fruits, such as mangoes, guavas and papayas.

Oranges are a medium-size fruit with a fine-grained skin, and popular varieties are Valencia, Jaffa and Shamouti, which is available only during the winter. They often

contain a lot of pips (seeds), which are high in pectin. Navel oranges are seedless, so are best preserved whole, either in segments or in slices. Red-flushed blood oranges have ruby-coloured flesh and a rich, almost berry-like flavour. Bitter Seville oranges have a high pectin and acid content, as well as an excellent, punchy flavour, and make the finest preserves.

Tangerines and mandarin oranges are small, flat citrus fruits with loose skins and a sweet or tart-sweet flavour. Satsumas, clementines and mineolas also fall into this group.

TROPICAL FRUITS

With imports from many parts of the world, tropical fruits are now available all year round, but tend to be at their best during the winter months. They are often vibrantly coloured with fabulous flavours and make fragrant savoury jellies and luxurious chutneys.

Pineapples have extremely juicy, sweet and refreshing golden flesh. They can be made into crisp-textured relishes, which are ideal for serving with chicken, pork and ham. Once picked, pineapples do not ripen, so always buy ripe fruits.

Guavas have a sweet, almost spicy aroma and flavour, with granular flesh that becomes creamy when ripe. Peel them thinly, then halve and remove the seeds. It is essential to add lemon or lime juice to preserves that are made with guavas to achieve a good set and to heighten the flavour.

Left: Fragrant mangoes are fabulous made into sweet and tangy chutney.

Left: Limes have a distinctive, sharp flavour and are delicious made into salty pickles.

Papayas, also known as pawpaw, are pear-shaped fruits which have soft flesh and a green skin that turns a speckled yellow when the fruit is ripe. Use slightly under-ripe fruits to make chutneys.

Mangoes have deep-orange flesh, which will yield slightly when the uncut fruit is gently squeezed. Just-ripe and green under-ripe mangoes can be made into excellent, highly flavoured chutneys and pickles. When mangoes are scarce or expensive, substitute up to half the total weight with cooking apples.

Pomegranate seeds, pith and membranes are bitter and it is the juice that is extracted to make savoury jellies and relishes. The simplest way to do this is to cut the fruit in half and use a lemon squeezer, taking care not to crush the seeds. Grenadine, a sweet syrup used in cocktails and mixed drinks, is made from pomegranate juice, and a dash of this can be used to flavour preserves.

OTHER FRUITS

Grape flavours range from honey-sweet to sharp and almost lemon-scented. The smaller seedless grapes are preferable for preserves as they need less preparation and have thin skins with little tannin. They can be pickled or included in chutneys and relishes.

Melons come in two kinds: the dessert melon and the watermelon. The flavour of dessert melon is not intense and is most often combined with strong flavours such as ginger, or other fruits. Watermelon flesh has a high water content so it is rarely used in preserves. The skin can be diced and pickled.

Dates are plump and glossy and packed with concentrated sugar. The thin papery skins should be slipped off and the long stone (pit) removed before the flesh is added to chutneys. When the date is squeezed at the stem end, the flesh should pop out of the skin, then you can use a sharp knife to cut the fruit in half and carefully prise out the stone. The sweet flavour of dates combines very well with vinegar to make a wonderful sweet-and-sour preserve that goes particularly well with cheese. Semi-dried and dried dates are also widely available and can be added to chutneys.

Rhubarb is available in late spring, has crimson and green stems and can be made into chutney. It has a very sharp, intense flavour and goes well with orange and ginger.

Figs are fragile fruits which require careful handling. They have thin skins that may be purple or greenish gold and a glorious soft, scented flesh filled with tiny seeds. They can be used fresh or dried to make luxurious chutneys. Warm spices such as cinnamon, nutmeg and vanilla go very well with figs.

Right: The bright pink juice of pomegranates can be made into beautiful glistening savoury jellies.

DRIED FRUITS

All kinds of fruits are available dried and they can successfully be made into pickles. Less sugar is needed than with fresh fruit and pre-soaking is unnecessary; the fruit is put straight into sterilized bottles and hot vinegar poured over.

Dried fruits are also good when added to chutneys, especially when vegetables with a high water content such as marrows (large zucchini) and squashes are used. The dried fruits help to soak up the excess liquid, add flavour and speed up the time it takes the chutney to thicken. The shorter cooking time helps to retain the fresh flavour of the other ingredients. Raisins, sultanas (golden raisins) and currants are often added to chutneys to give a sweet-and-sour result.

VEGETABLE FRUITS

Sweet (bell) peppers, tomatoes and aubergines (eggplants) are fruits, but they are treated like vegetables.

THE PEPPER FAMILY

From mild peppers to hot chillies, this family of vegetable fruits can be preserved in pickles, chutneys or relishes, or used to add flavour and texture to preserves made with a variety of other vegetables.
Sweet peppers are the mildest members of the capsicum family. Young peppers have a sharp flavour and are bright green. As they mature, they become sweeter and turn yellow, then orange and finally red. Preserved green peppers tend to lose their colour with long-term storage, which is unimportant in dark chutneys, but best avoided in clear pickles.

Chillies These small, potent peppers are the world's most popular spice. Green chillies are immature, while red ones are ripe. As a general rule, chillies sweeten as they ripen and heat is influenced by a combination of variety and the climate. Anaheim and Dutch chillies are mild, jalapeño and Scotch bonnets are hotter, and tiny Thai or bird's eye chillies are very hot. Dried chillies are used in most pickling spices.

TOMATOES

Ripe tomatoes may be yellow or red, depending on variety, and their sweetness or acidity varies according to type and how ripe they were when picked. The common round tomato is juicy and fairly acidic. Italian plum tomatoes have an elongated shape, denser flesh and a sweeter flavour. Cherry tomatoes are tiny and very sweet, while beefsteak tomatoes can weigh up to 450g/1lb. Unripe green tomatoes, picked at the end of the season, are often made into green tomato chutney, but may also be included in tart relishes such as piccalilli. They are slightly bland, so they are best combined with other fruit and vegetables and plenty of flavourings.

If the tomatoes are not going to be strained after cooking, their tough skins should be removed before cooking; the easiest way to do this is to blanch them first. Ripe tomatoes can also be dried in the oven, then bottled in oil.

Left: Crisp green peppers are good in dark-coloured relishes.

Above: Tomatoes have tough skins so are often better peeled before adding to pickles and preserves.

Choose firm, unblemished tomatoes, preferably with the calyx intact. Once ripe, they should be preserved as soon as possible. They can be stored in the salad drawer of the refrigerator for a few days.

AUBERGINES/EGGPLANTS

The most common aubergines are large, oval and dark purple, but there are also smaller, round, purple ones and a little oval, ivory-white variety that inspired the American name eggplant. Aubergines may be pickled raw, either sliced or whole, but they are more usually chopped and cooked in pickles. They are often salted when making chutneys and pickles to extract some of the moisture, which would otherwise dilute the mixture. When buying, look for small to medium-sized aubergines with smooth, shiny skins rather than larger, more mature specimens. Aubergines can be stored in the refrigerator for up to two weeks before preserving.

THE ONION FAMILY

These pungent, punchy vegetables vary in size and intensity. From small, crunchy, potent pickling onions to large, mild leeks, members of this diverse family form the basis of a great many pickles, relishes and chutneys.

Onions This versatile vegetable family includes strongly flavoured brown-skinned onions, used for everyday cooking, and the larger mild, sweet and juicy Spanish onions which are also known as yellow or Bermuda onions. White onions with papery skins and colourful red onions are mild and sweet. All types can be made into onion chutneys and relishes, sliced and pickled in rings, or dried.

Pickling onions, also called button or pearl onions, have brown papery skins. They are main-crop onions, picked when very small. Milder, smaller silverskin onions, which are harvested when they have a diameter of no more than 2.5cm/1in, can also be pickled.

Soaking them in a wet brine for 24–36 hours draws out some of the moisture and gives them a crunchier texture when pickled. It is important to use a stainless steel knife when preparing onions to prevent the cut surfaces from darkening.

Shallots These are a different variety of onion, grown in clusters rather than as single bulbs. They have an elongated shape and papery russet skin. Shallots have a fuller, sweeter flavour than onions and are delicious pickled.

Spring onions are also known as green onions or scallions. Usually used in salads, these are tender young bulb onions, pulled while the tops are still green and before the bulb has had a chance to swell. Long cooking does not suit spring onions, so they are rarely used

Above: Shallots have a strong flavour and are very good pickled in malt or cider vinegar.

in chutneys. They may, however, be pickled whole or chopped and added to relishes and chutneys with short cooking times.

Leeks Long, thin leeks are the mildest members of the onion family. They are included in chutneys to add texture and flavour, or pickled on their own. To clean leeks, slit them lengthways and rinse under cold water to remove any trapped grit.

Garlic This is the most pungent member of the onion family. One or two cloves can be used to add a subtle flavour to chutney and relishes. Vinegar can be flavoured with garlic, then used to make preserves; peel the cloves and add 5 or 6 to each 600ml/1 pint/ 2½ cups vinegar. Leave for 2 weeks to infuse and use within 4 months.

PEELING PICKLING ONIONS

1 Place the onions in a bowl and pour over boiling water to cover. Leave for 1–2 minutes.

2 Drain the onions and rinse under cold water to cool. Using a sharp knife, trim the tops and root end, then slip the skins from the onions.

OTHER VEGETABLES

A huge range of vegetables are used for making preserves and chutneys, and all add their own individual texture, colour and flavour.

MUSHROOMS

The common cultivated mushroom is sold at various stages in its growth. Button (white) mushrooms are the youngest and the best for pickling and preserving. When the cap has partially opened, they are sold as cup mushrooms and, when opened out completely, as flat or Portabello mushrooms. The larger they grow, the more flavour they have and the darker their juices. Buy fresh firm-textured mushrooms and preserve promptly after buying. Wipe them clean with a damp cloth and wash only if very dirty; do not leave mushrooms to soak.

ROOTS

Roots tend to become starchier with age, so they are usually preserved while young, sweet and tender.
Beetroot/beet Dark ruby-red beetroot has a rich, sweet flavour and is one of the most commonly preserved root vegetables. There are two varieties of beetroot: globe and a long, slender variety. The former is usually preserved whole and the latter sliced into rounds. When preparing beetroot, be careful not to damage the skin, or the colour will leach out. Trim the stalks to 2.5cm/1in above the root. When pickling whole, choose small, tender even-size beetroot that need the same cooking time.
Parsnips, swedes/rutabagas and turnips Creamy-coloured parsnips should be scrubbed before preserving and peeled if tough. Use young vegetables because large roots can be woody. The globe-shaped swede has creamy, orange flesh and a delicate flavour. Turnips are smaller than swede and they have white flesh with a peppery taste.

SQUASHES

There are two main categories of this vegetable: winter squash, which include pumpkins and butternut squash; and summer squash, which include marrows/large zucchini, cucumber and courgettes/zucchini. Most are now available all year round.

Left: Tender, crunchy baby turnips are excellent pickled.

Above: Flat mushrooms are perfect for making into mushroom ketchup.

Winter squashes have tough inedible skins, large seeds and dense fibrous flesh which can be used to add sweetness and a rich orange colour to chutneys.
Marrows are known as large zucchini in the United States, and have a high water content so they are best brined before making into chutney.
Cucumbers are also usually brined before preserving. As a rule, small ridged cucumbers are pickled; long salad ones are used in relishes.
Courgettes/zucchini have a dark green shiny skin with light streaks and are pickled when small.

Below: Butternut squash is great added to chutneys and pickles.

BRASSICAS

This family of vegetables ranges from leafy cabbages to creamy cauliflowers.

Cabbages come in a variety of forms; from dark green, crinkly-leafed Savoy to tightly wrapped white cabbages. Firm white and red cabbages are most suitable for preserving. Red cabbage is similar to white cabbage in texture, but has a sweeter taste and takes slightly longer to cook. If it needs to be blanched before preserving, add a little vinegar to the water to help to retain the red colour.

Cauliflower The white florets of this mild-flavoured brassica soak up spices well and so are often used in hot and spicy Indian pickles and chutneys. When buying, check that the florets are not discoloured and that the remaining leaves are fresh and green, not yellow and wilted.

Broccoli is not often used in chutneys because it tends to discolour when stored, but you can cut it into tiny florets and add towards the end of the cooking time in piccalilli and relishes which will be eaten quickly.

SHOOTS

These tender vegetables have mild but distinctive flavours.

Asparagus can be included in luxurious preserves. It should be used when very fresh; the stalks should be firm and the tips plump.

Celery may have white or green stalks, which should snap easily. Celery does not make a good pickle on its own, but is often added to mixed pickles, chutneys and relishes. Wrapped in a plastic bag, celery will keep in the refrigerator for a week or more.

Globe artichokes These look like enormous thistle-heads with purple-tinged green leaves. They are

Above: Broad beans, runner beans and French beans can all be added to chutneys and preserves.

difficult to preserve whole, but the hearts can be pickled in a mild vinegar, such as white wine or cider (hard cider) vinegar, then drizzled with olive oil to serve.

PODS AND SEEDS

This group of vegetables includes peas, beans and corn.

Peas in their pods have a sweet flavour and make a tasty addition to chutneys and relishes. Add them 10 minutes before the end of the cooking time, so that they retain their texture and colour.

Green beans French beans are narrow green beans with round pods that are available all year round; American green beans are similar, but larger. Flat runner beans are popular in Britain and are at their best in summer. Trim beans before use; some varieties of runner beans, and particularly older ones, may need stringing.

MAKING SAUERKRAUT
This classic pickled cabbage from Germany has a sharp, pungent flavour that goes very well with meats and cheeses.

1 Finely shred 1.2kg/2½lb white cabbage. Toss it with 25g/1oz coarse kosher salt and 7.5ml/1½ tsp spices such as caraway seeds, crushed juniper berries and black peppercorns. Leave to stand for about 10 minutes, mix again, then pack into a large sterilized crock or bowl.

2 Weight the cabbage with a large plate, cover the crock or bowl with a lid and leave it in a cool place (below 20°C/70°F) for 1 week.

3 Remove the plate and skim off any scum with a spoon. Repeat daily for about 1 month until no more scum appears. (This means that the cabbage is ready.)

4 Pack into sterilized jars, cover and store in the refrigerator for up to 1 month.

HERBS

Herbs are an essential part of most preserves and using the right amount is as important as selecting the correct one. In some preserves a subtle hint is all that is needed; in others the flavouring is one of the main ingredients.

Fresh and dried herbs are invaluable in savoury preserves. They can be added during the initial cooking, then removed, or finely chopped and stirred in towards the end of cooking. If dried herbs are used instead of fresh, then reduce the quantity by between a third and a half.

Below: Oregano has a lovely, aromatic flavour that is very good with summer squashes.

TENDER HERBS

Herbs with fragile leaves need careful handling to avoid bruising. Once picked, they should be used within a few days.

Mint The many varieties of this aromatic herb include peppermint, spearmint, apple mint, lemon mint and pineapple mint. It adds a fresh flavour to preserves, but should be used sparingly.

Parsley Curly and flat leaf varieties are available. It is an essential herb in a bouquet garni.

Tarragon This herb is excellent for flavouring vinegars but is rarely used in its fresh form because it darkens and discolours on heating.

ROBUST HERBS

Often woody, with pungent leaves, these herbs are added to preserves during cooking to extract and mellow their flavour.

Bay leaves Essential in bouquet garni, these dark green glossy leaves should be dried for a few days before use. They add a slightly spicy flavour to preserves.

Marjoram and oregano Popular in tomato preserves, these herbs are also good with marrow (large zucchini). They should be added towards the end of cooking.

Rosemary Powerfully aromatic, fresh or dried rosemary should be used in small quantities. It goes very well with citrus fruits.

Sage is a strong herb that often partners garlic and tomatoes.

Thyme This robust herb works well with preserves made from roasted vegetables and beans.

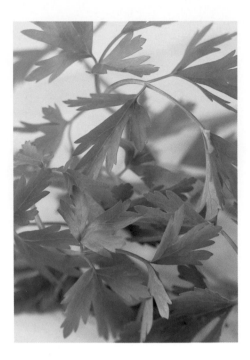

Above: Parsley has a mild flavour and is often used with other herbs.

AROMATIC AND SPICY HERBS

Some herbs have aromatic citrus flavours, others aniseed tones; a few have a warm, spicy pungency.

Coriander/cilantro Every part of this aromatic herb can be used. Also known as Chinese parsley, the leaves resemble slightly rounded flat leaf parsley. They have a warm, spicy taste and add pungency to Middle Eastern, Asian and Indian chutneys and fresh, Mexican-style relishes.

Dill This delicate herb has dark green, feathery leaves and a subtle aniseed taste. It is an excellent flavouring for courgette (zucchini) and cucumber relishes and pickles.

Fennel is similar to dill, but has a stronger flavour and is particularly good for flavouring vinegars.

Lemon grass A tall hard grass, with a distinctive lemony aroma and taste, lemon grass is often used in Thai preserves and should be bruised to release the flavour.

SPICES

These can be hot and spicy or warm and fragrant. Store spices in a cool, dark place: ground ones will keep for up to six months, whole spices for a year.

HOT SPICES

These spices can be mild and subtle or exceedingly fiery.
Cayenne is made from ground dried chillies, is extremely hot and should be used sparingly.
Chillies Fresh chillies may be cooked in preserves to add heat, or added whole or chopped to clear pickles when bottling.
Ginger Root ginger may be used fresh, dried or ground in all kinds of preserves.
Mustard There are three types of mustard seed: white, brown and black; the latter is the hottest.

Below: Sweet, mild paprika is used to add both flavour and colour to chutneys and relishes.

Whole mustard seeds are often included in pickles, and ground mustard powder in relishes.
Paprika This rich, red spice is sold ground and its flavour ranges from mild and sweet to strong and pungent.
Peppercorns Often added whole to pickles, these tiny round berries may be green, black or white. Green ones are mildly flavoured, black ones are hot and pungent and white ones have a mild aromatic flavour.
Turmeric has a warm, spicy taste and is often used simply for its colour in pickles and relishes.

SEED SPICES

Some plants are grown for their seeds alone; others, such as coriander and dill, are cultivated for both their leaves and seeds.
Coriander seeds These small round seeds have a mild-orange flavour and taste different from the green leafy herb. They are usually included in pickling spice.
Dill seeds Small oval seeds with a similar flavour to caraway, these are often used with cucumber pickles and relishes.

FRAGRANT SPICES

Spices with a warm, fragrant flavour work very well when used in preserves containing fruit.
Allspice Similar in aroma and flavour to cinammon, cloves and nutmeg, this is good used with orchard fruits.
Cassia and cinnamon The bark of evergreen trees, these are available ground or in sticks.

Right: Fresh root ginger adds warmth and a lively fresh flavour to all kinds of preserves.

Cloves These tiny dried flower buds, sold whole or ground, have a distinctive taste that goes well with apples and citrus fruit.
Juniper Used to give gin its distinctive flavour, the blue-black berries can be used fresh or dried.
Star anise This star-shaped, aniseed-flavoured spice looks great in pickles and bottled preserves.

PICKLING SPICES

Various blends of pickling spices are available. Typical mixtures include allspice, bay leaf, cardamom, coriander and mustard seeds, cassia or cinnamon, dried chillies, whole cloves, dried root ginger and peppercorns. Add 5–15ml/1–3 tsp of pickling spices to each 600ml/1 pint/2½ cups vinegar and simmer for 5–15 minutes, then cool and strain.

GRINDING WHOLE SPICES
Spices may be bought ready-ground but most are best when freshly ground because, once ground, they quickly lose their flavour and aroma. Grind spices by hand using a mortar and pestle, or use a spice mill or coffee grinder reserved solely for this purpose.

EQUIPMENT

While very few specialist items are essential for preserving, having the correct equipment for the job helps to ensure success. You will probably have most of the basic items such as a large heavy pan, weighing scales or calibrated measuring cups, wooden spoons, a vegetable peeler, a chopping board and some sharp knives. However, a few specific items such as a salometer and a jelly bag will prove invaluable. The following are readily available from large department stores and specialist kitchen equipment stores.

PRESERVING PAN

A preserving pan or large, heavy pan is essential for making perfect preserves. It must be of a sufficient size to allow rapid boiling without bubbling over (a capacity of about 9 litres/16 pints/8 quarts is ideal); wide enough to allow rapid evaporation of liquid, so that setting point is reached quickly; and have a thick heavy base to protect the preserve from burning during cooking. A non-corrosive preserving pan such as one made of stainless steel is the best choice for making all types of preserves, but especially for pickles, chutneys and relishes that contain a high concentration of acid.

SUGAR THERMOMETER

Invaluable for cooking preserves to the exact temperature needed for a perfect set. Choose a thermometer that goes up to at least 110°C/ 230°F, and has a clip or a handle that can be attached to the pan, so that it does not slip into the boiling preserve.

JELLY BAG

Used to strain fruit juices from cooked fruit pulp for jelly-making, jelly bags are made from calico, cotton flannel or nylon. Some have their own stands; others have loops with which to suspend the bag.

MUSLIN/CHEESECLOTH

Muslin can be used for making spice, herb or jelly bags. To make a jelly bag, layer three squares of muslin together and tie lengths of string (twine) securely to each corner. Either knot the ends together to hang from a single support, or make four loops so the bag can be suspended on the legs of an upturned stool or chair.

Below: A selection of jars with clamp-top, screw-top or two-piece screw-band lids.

JARS AND BOTTLES

When making pickles, chutneys and relishes, a selection of containers is needed. Clear glass is ideal because it is non-corrosive, you can easily check for trapped air bubbles and it looks very pretty when filled. As well as ordinary jam jars and bottles, there are specialist preserving jars that are designed to be heated to a high temperature. Non-corrosive seals are essential, particularly when potting acidic chutneys and pickles.

Wide-necked jars are crucial for recipes using whole or large pieces of fruit or vegetables, but for most preserves it is better to use several smaller jars than one or two large ones.

PRESERVE COVERS

Waxed paper and cellophane, secured by an elastic band, can be used to cover jellies, but paper and cellophane are not vinegar-proof so are unsuitable for preserves containing vinegar. These should be potted in preserving jars with acid-resistant seals or jam jars with plastic-lined lids.

HYDROMETER

A hydrometer measures the density of sugar syrup and can be used when making a range of preserves, savoury jellies and relishes. The tube is marked from 0 to 40 and measures the point to which the weighted tube sinks. The more sugar a syrup contains, the higher the hydrometer will float in it.

Right: A canelle knife and zester are excellent for paring off thin strips of citrus rind for pickles and relishes.

SALOMETER

This works in the same way as a hydrometer but is used to measure the amount of salt dissolved in brine for pickling. Salometers are marked from 0 to 100.

SIEVES AND COLANDERS

Use nylon, plastic or stainless steel sieves and colanders when straining acidic fruit or preserves.

SLOTTED SPOONS AND SKIMMERS

These are useful for lifting and draining solid ingredients and packing them into jars.

ZESTERS

The cutting edge of a zester has five little holes, which, when pulled firmly across the fruit, remove fine strands of citrus rind, leaving the white pith behind. This is ideal for relishes and chutneys that are flavoured with citrus rind.

CANELLE KNIVES

These have a v-shaped tooth that pares 6mm/¼in strips of peel from fruit and vegetables leaving grooves and creating a striped effect.

GRATERS

Box graters usually have a choice of at least three different surfaces, from fine (for nutmeg and lemon rind) to coarse (for hard fruits and vegetables).

MINCERS/GRINDERS AND FOOD MILLS

Both hand and electric mincers can save a good deal of time and energy when processing large quantities of fruit or vegetables.

GRINDERS

The mortar and pestle is perfect for coarsely grinding small quantities of spices. For larger amounts or when a fine powder is required, use a spice mill or coffee grinder kept solely for that purpose.

Left: A box grater with several different surfaces is useful for preparing fruits, vegetables and spices.

POTTING AND BOTTLING

Make sure you have enough jars and bottles and the correct sterilizing equipment before you start to make any preserve.

CHOOSING CONTAINERS

Pickles made from whole or large pieces of fruit or vegetables should be packed into medium or large jars or bottles with a wide neck. Smooth, pourable sauces or relishes can be stored in narrow-necked bottles, but thicker, spoonable preserves should be packed in jars.

STERILIZING JARS AND BOTTLES

Before potting, it is essential to sterilize jars and bottles to destroy any micro-organisms in containers.

Check jars and bottles for cracks or damage, then wash in hot, soapy water, rinse and turn upside-down to drain. Containers may be sterilized in five different ways: by heating in a low oven, using sterilizing tablets, hot-washing in a dishwasher, immersing in boiling water, or heating in a microwave.

oven method

Stand the containers, spaced slightly apart, on a baking sheet lined with kitchen paper. Rest any lids on top. Place in a cold oven, then heat to 110°C/225°F/Gas ¼ and bake for 30 minutes.

sterilizing tablet method

This method is not suitable for delicately flavoured preserves. Following the instructions on the packet, dissolve the tablets and soak the containers in the sterilizing solution. Drain and dry before use.

Below: Medium, wide-necked jars with plastic-coated screw-top lids are ideal for most preserves.

dishwasher method

Put the containers and lids in a dishwasher and run it on its hottest setting, including drying.

boiling water method

1 Place the containers, open-end up, in a deep pan in one layer.

2 Pour enough hot (but not boiling) water into the pan to cover the containers. Bring the water to the boil and boil for 10 minutes.

3 Leave in the pan until the water stops bubbling, then carefully remove and drain upside-down on a clean dishtowel. Turn the containers upright and leave to air-dry for a few minutes.

4 Immerse lids, seals and corks in simmering water for 20 seconds. (Only ever use corks once.)

microwave method

Follow the microwave manufacturer's instructions and only use for jars that hold less than 450g/1lb and short squat bottles.

1 Half fill the clean jars or bottles with water and heat on full power until the water has boiled for at least 1 minute.

2 Using oven gloves, remove the jars or bottles from the microwave. Carefully swirl the water inside them, then pour it away. Drain upside-down on a clean dishtowel, then turn upright and leave to dry.

Left: Preserves stored in clamp-top and two-piece lidded jars make very attractive gifts.

1 Using a ladle and funnel, fill the hot sterilized bottles to within 2.5cm/1in of the top.

2 Soak the corks in very hot water for 3–4 minutes, then push into the tops of the bottles as far as they will go. Gently tap the cork into the bottle using a rolling pin or wooden mallet until the cork is within 5mm/¼in of the top of the bottle. Leave the bottles until cold.

3 To seal, dip the top of each bottle in melted candle or sealing wax to coat. Leave to set, then dip a second time.

FILLING JARS AND BOTTLES

Most preserves should be potted into hot containers as soon as they are ready. Savoury jellies with added ingredients such as fresh herbs should be left to cool for 10 minutes until a thin skin forms on the surface. Some preserves such as fruits bottled in alcohol or vegetables preserved in vinegar are potted when cold rather than hot.

SEALING JARS

Different preserves need to be covered and sealed in different ways. Jellies can be covered with a waxed paper disc and the jar covered with cellophane held in place with an elastic band. Pickled vegetables must be sealed in jars with new rubber seals and vacuum or clamp top lids. Chutneys and pickles should be sealed in jars with vinegar-proof lids.

using lidded jars

Different types of jars are suitable for different types of preserves. **Screw-top lidded jars** are suitable for most preserves, although those with uncoated metal lids should be avoided when potting acidic preserves containing vinegar because the lid may corrode. **Two-piece lidded jars** are also known as lid and screw-band jars. They consist of a flat rubber- or plastic-coated lid that fits exactly over the top of the jar and a ring that screws on to the neck of the jar to hold the lid in place. **Clamp-top jars** can be used for any kind of preserve.

FILLING AND SEALING BOTTLES

Bottles are perfect for storing sauces and pourable relishes. They can be stoppered with a sterilized cork, then dipped in wax to seal.

PRESENTATION

Glass jars and bottles look pretty because they allow you to see the preserve inside. Preserving jars are practical and attractive for savoury preserves, while glazed earthenware pots are good for storing chutneys and mustards.

LABELLING PRESERVES

All preserves should be clearly labelled with the date, the name of the preserve and any special notes.

STORING PRESERVES

Preserves should always be kept in a cool, dark, dry place because warmth and light will affect their colour and flavour and shorten their shelf-life. Many pickles, chutneys and bottled fruits need time to mature before being used.

HOW TO MAKE PICKLES

Pickles can be sharp, sweet or a combination of the two. They are made by preserving raw or lightly cooked fruit or vegetables in spiced vinegar. They may be eaten alone or as a condiment with cheese or cold meat. There are two types of pickles: clear pickles or sweet pickles. To make clear pickles such as pickled onions, salt or brine is used to extract water from the vegetables to give them a crisp texture before they are bottled in vinegar. To make sweet pickles, fruit or vegetables are usually cooked until tender, then bottled in a sweet vinegar syrup.

Fruit and vegetables used for pickling should be firm and young. Small varieties such as baby (pearl) onions, beetroot (beets), gherkins, plums and cherries, which can be pickled whole, are particularly good. Large vegetables such as cucumbers, marrows (large zucchini), cabbage and cauliflower should be sliced or chopped.

Most pickles have to be matured in a cool dark place for a minimum of 3 weeks and preferably for at least 2 months to develop and mellow their flavour before eating. Pickled cabbage loses its crisp texture after 2–3 months, so it should be eaten within 2 months of making.

Take care when packing the fruit or vegetables into jars – they should be packed well, but not too tightly because the vinegar must surround each piece. It is important to fill jars to the brim and avoid trapping air in the pickles because this will cause discoloration and may encourage the growth of bacteria and moulds.

Large, wide-necked jars are recommended for pickling. Screw-top jars with lids that have plastic-coated linings such as those used for commercial pickles are an ideal choice. Vinegar reacts with metal, causing it to corrode and flavour the pickle, so metal tops should always be avoided when pickling.

CLEAR PICKLES

When making clear pickles, the ingredients are usually prepared first by soaking them in a brine. The salt draws out the moisture from the vegetables, making them more receptive to vinegar and preventing vegetable juices from diluting the preserving vinegar. Pure or kosher salt should always be used because iodized salt will taint the pickle with an iodine flavour and the additives in table salt will make it cloudy. There are two types of brine: dry brine, where the salt is sprinkled over the vegetables; and wet brine, where the salt is dissolved in water first.

making pickled peppers using dry brine

For this method, salt is rubbed into the vegetables or, more simply, sprinkled between layers of vegetables to draw out the juices. This then produces a brine. Salting vegetables makes them firmer and crunchier. It is particularly suitable for vegetables with a high water content such as (bell) peppers. Other vegetables that suit this method include cucumbers and courgettes (zucchini).

Makes about 1.8kg/4lb

INGREDIENTS

1.3kg/3lb red and yellow (bell) peppers
60ml/4 tbsp salt
750ml/1¼ pints/3 cups distilled malt vinegar
2 fresh bay leaves
2 thyme sprigs
5ml/1 tsp black peppercorns

1 Wash the peppers and pat them dry on kitchen paper. Cut each one into quarters lengthways, remove the seeds and cores, then cut each quarter in half to make long wide strips. If the peppers are very large, cut each quarter into three strips rather than two.

2 Layer the peppers in a large, non-corrosive bowl, fleshy side up, lightly sprinkling salt between each layer. Cover the bowl with clear film (plastic wrap) and leave to stand in a cool place for 8 hours or overnight to extract the moisture. If the weather is warm, place the bowl in the refrigerator.

3 Tip the peppers into a colander or large sieve and rinse thoroughly in cold water to remove the salt. The easiest way to check for salt is to taste one of the peppers: if it is too salty, rinse again.

4 Drain the peppers well and pat dry with kitchen paper. This is important because excess water will dilute the vinegar.

5 Pour the vinegar into a pan and add the herbs and peppercorns. Slowly bring to the boil, then simmer for 2 minutes.

6 Meanwhile, pack the peppers into hot sterilized jars. Remove the herbs from the pickling vinegar and tuck them into the jars.

7 Pour the vinegar and peppercorns over the peppers, filling the jars almost up to the brim. (To make an even crunchier pickle, allow the vinegar to cool first.)

8 Gently tap the jars on the work surface to release any trapped air bubbles, then seal with vinegar-proof lids. Store in a cool, dark place for 4 weeks before eating. Use within 1 year.

making vegetable pickle using wet brine

For this method, salt is mixed with water to make a brine solution. The ingredients are then immersed in the brine, sometimes for several days before pickling in vinegar. Wet brine may be used hot but it is more often used cold. For most pickles, a 10 per cent salt solution is used; this requires 50g/2oz/¼ cup salt to every 600ml/1 pint/2½ cups water. In some preserves where vinegar is used with sugar, this may be reduced to a 5 per cent solution.

Pickling using wet brine is suitable for ingredients with a very dense texture or thick skin such as whole lemons, watermelon rind and green walnuts, or where a softer result is required.

Makes about 1.3kg/3lb

INGREDIENTS
1.3kg/3lb mixed vegetables such as baby (pearl) onions, carrots, cauliflower and green beans

175g/6oz/¾ cup salt

1.75 litres/3 pints/7½ cups water

2 bay leaves

0.75–1 litre/1¼–1¾ pints/3–4 cups spiced vinegar

1 Prepare the vegetables: skin, peel, and trim as necessary. Leave the onions whole, thickly slice the carrots, break the cauliflower into small florets and cut the beans into 2.5cm/1in lengths. Place the vegetables in a large glass bowl.

2 Put the salt and water in a large pan and warm over a low heat until the salt has dissolved completely. Leave to cool, then pour enough over the prepared vegetables to cover completely.

3 Place a plate, slightly smaller than the diameter of the bowl, on top of the vegetables to keep them submerged in the brine. Leave to stand for 24 hours.

4 Tip the vegetables into a colander or sieve to drain, then rinse well in cold water to remove the excess brine. Drain again and pat dry using kitchen paper.

5 Put the bay leaves and vinegar in a pan and slowly bring to the boil over a low heat.

6 Meanwhile, pack the brined vegetables into hot sterilized jars. Tuck in the bay leaves and pour in the hot vinegar, filling the jars almost to the top.

7 Gently tap the jars to release any trapped air bubbles, cover and seal. Store the vegetables in a cool, dark place for 4 weeks before eating. Use within 1 year.

making unbrined pickled mushrooms

Not all clear pickles are brined before bottling in vinegar. The moisture can be removed from mushrooms by simmering them gently in water with a little salt until just tender. This method is also suitable for beetroot (beets).

Makes about 450g/1lb

INGREDIENTS

1 small onion
1 garlic clove
300ml/½ pint/1¼ cups
    white wine vinegar
6 black peppercorns
sprig of fresh thyme
275g/10oz/3¼ cups small button
    (white) mushrooms
600ml/1 pint/2½ cups water
10ml/2 tsp salt

1 Thinly slice the onion and bruise the garlic clove and place in a pan with the vinegar, peppercorns and thyme. Bring the mixture slowly to the boil over a low heat, then half cover the pan with a lid. Simmer for 15 minutes. Remove from the heat, cover completely with the lid and leave to cool.

2 Meanwhile, wipe the mushrooms clean with damp kitchen paper and trim the stems if necessary.

3 Place the mushrooms in a pan with the water and salt. Bring to the boil and simmer for 1 minute. Remove from the heat, cover and leave to cool for 4 minutes, stirring a couple of times, so that all sides of the mushrooms are immersed in the hot water.

4 Tip the mushrooms into a colander or sieve, leave to drain, then pat dry using kitchen paper.

5 Pack the mushrooms into clean sterilized jars, then strain the vinegar mixture into the jars, covering the mushrooms and filling the jars almost to the top.

6 Seal the jars and store in a cool dark place for at least 3 weeks before eating. Use within 1 year.

PICKLING GREEN VEGETABLES
The colour of green vegetables tends to be lost if stored for more than a few months, although their flavour remains the same. Blanching them in boiling water mixed with 5ml/ 1 tsp bicarbonate of soda (baking soda) for 30 seconds helps to retain their colour, but destroys the vitamin C content.

SPICED PICKLING VINEGAR

Ready-spiced pickling vinegar and jars or packets of mixed pickling spices are readily available from supermarkets. However, you can make your own, adapting the combination of spices according to personal preference and the ingredients to be preserved. You can use any variety of vinegar, but make sure that it has an acetic acid content of at least 5 per cent.

making basic spiced pickling vinegar

Makes 1.2 litres/2 pints/5 cups

INGREDIENTS

15ml/1 tbsp allspice berries
15ml/1 tbsp cloves
5cm/2in piece fresh root ginger, peeled
    and sliced
1 cinnamon stick
12 whole black peppercorns
1.2 litres/2 pints/5 cups vinegar

1 Put all the spices in a jar and pour over the vinegar. Cover the jar and leave to steep for 1–2 months, shaking occasionally.

2 After this time, strain the vinegar and return it to the cleaned jar and store it in a cool dark place until ready to use.

COOK'S TIP
To make quick pickling vinegar for immediate use, put all the ingredients in a pan and heat gently to boiling point. Simmer for about 1 minute, then remove from the heat, cover and leave to infuse (steep) for 1 hour. Strain and use.

SWEET PICKLES

For these pickles, fruit and some vegetables such as cucumbers are preserved in sweetened vinegar. They are excellent served as an accompaniment to cold meats, poultry and cheeses. Pickled apples or pears are also delicious served with hot baked ham or grilled (broiled) meat such as lamb chops. Sweet pickles are always made with distilled malt, wine or cider vinegar rather than brown malt vinegar, which would overpower the flavour and affect the colour of the fruit.

To offset the sharpness of the vinegar, a fairly large amount of sugar is added, usually between 350g/12oz/scant 1¾ cups and 450g/1lb/2¼ cups to every 300ml/½ pint/1¼ cups vinegar. Unlike vegetables, fruits do not need to be brined before pickling. Fruits that are pickled whole such as plums and cherries should be pricked before the initial cooking to allow the vinegar syrup to penetrate the skin and stop the fruit shrivelling. Some fruits such as berries become very soft when pickled and are therefore better preserved in sugar syrup or alcohol.

Spices and flavourings add zest to sweet pickles. They are best infused in the vinegar at the start of cooking, but also look attractive added to the bottle when packing the preserve. Use whole spices such as cinnamon, cloves, allspice, ginger, nutmeg and mace; ground spices will make the pickle murky. Citrus rind and vanilla pods (beans) also add a wonderful taste and aroma. Robustly flavoured herbs such as rosemary and bay leaves work well in sweet pickles.

making pickled apples

Makes about 1.3kg/3lb

INGREDIENTS

750ml/1¼ pints/3 cups raspberry, cider or white wine vinegar

1 cinnamon stick

5cm/2in piece fresh root ginger, peeled and sliced

6 whole cloves

1.3kg/3lb eating apples, peeled, cored and halved

800g/1¾lb/4 cups granulated sugar

1 Put the vinegar in a stainless steel pan with the cinnamon, ginger and cloves, and bring to the boil. Reduce the heat and simmer gently for about 5 minutes.

2 Add the apples to the vinegar and simmer for 5–10 minutes until they are almost tender. Be careful not to overcook the fruit; it will continue to cook in the hot syrup and should still be firm when packed into the jars.

3 Using a slotted spoon, lift the apples out of the vinegar and pack them into hot sterilized jars, adding the cloves and the cinnamon stick, if you like.

4 Add the sugar to the vinegar and heat gently over a low heat, stirring until dissolved completely.

5 Increase the heat and boil the syrup rapidly for 5 minutes, or until the syrup has reduced and thickened slightly.

6 Strain the syrup through a sieve into a jug (pitcher), then pour it over the apples to cover them completely. Seal and label. Store the jars in a cool dark place and use within 1 year.

RASPBERRY VINEGAR

Fruit vinegars are perfect for making sweet pickles and are very easy to make at home.

To make about 750ml/1¼ pints/3 cups raspberry vinegar, put 450g/1lb/generous 2½ cups fresh raspberries in a bowl with 600ml/1 pint/2½ cups white wine or cider vinegar. Cover the bowl with a cloth and leave in a cool place for 4–5 days, stirring each day.

Strain the vinegar through a nylon or stainless-steel sieve and discard the raspberries. Pour the liquid into a jelly bag suspended over a large bowl or jug (pitcher). Leave to drain, then pour the vinegar into sterilized bottles and seal. Store in a cool dark place and use within 1 year.

PICKLING DRIED FRUITS

All sorts of dried fruits can be made into excellent pickles. The fruits soak up the pickling syrup, becoming soft, succulent and juicy. Dried apricots, peaches, pears, figs, prunes and mango slices are all perfect for pickling.

Pickles made with dried fruit do not need as much sugar as pickles made with fresh fruit; dried fruits are already packed with sugar. A small amount of liquid such as apple juice or water may be used to rehydrate the fruit before pickling. This prevents the fruit soaking up too much vinegar and the flavour becoming overpowering.

When pickling light-coloured dried fruits such as apricots, pears or apples, use light-coloured sugars and vinegars. Dark-coloured fruits such as figs and prunes can be pickled using malt or red wine vinegar and darker sugars.

SWEET PICKLING VINEGAR
When choosing vinegar for sweet pickles, it is important to think about the colour as well as the flavour of the vinegar. For green fruits such as green figs or red fruits such as plums, choose a light-coloured vinegar and spices or flavourings that won't alter the colour. Using a dark vinegar will turn the fruits a sludgy brown colour. Yellow fruits such as nectarines and apricots, and white or creamy fruits such as pears look stunning pickled in a coloured vinegar such as raspberry.

making pickled prunes

Makes about 1.3kg/3lb

INGREDIENTS

675g/1½lb/3 cups prunes

150ml/¼ pint/⅔ cup clear apple juice

750ml/1¼ pints/3 cups pickling malt vinegar

strip of pared orange rind

350g/12oz/1½ cups light muscovado (brown) sugar

1 Put the prunes in a non-corrosive pan, pour over the apple juice and cover. Leave to soak for 2 hours, or until the prunes have absorbed most of the juice.

2 Uncover the pan, add the vinegar and orange rind and bring slowly to the boil over a gentle heat. Reduce the heat and simmer gently for 10–15 minutes until the prunes are plump and juicy.

3 Remove the strip of orange rind from the pan and discard. Using a slotted spoon, lift the prunes out of the vinegar and pack well into hot sterilized jars.

4 Add the sugar to the vinegar and heat gently, stirring, until the sugar has dissolved completely. Bring the mixture to a rapid boil and cook for about 5 minutes, or until slightly reduced and thickened.

5 Carefully pour the hot vinegar syrup over the prunes and seal. Store in a cool dark place for at least 2 weeks before eating. Use within 1 year.

USING DRIED FRUITS IN PRESERVES
Dried fruits can be used in many types of preserve. They absorb liquid readily, so are often added to chutneys to help thicken the mixture. Raisins and sultanas (golden raisins) are particularly popular for this. Chopped dried apricots, peaches, dates and figs can also be used and contribute a substantial texture as well as a lovely sweet flavour.

Dried fruit is widely used to impart a full, fruity flavour to cooked relishes and savoury preserves made with mildly flavoured vegetables such as pumpkin, squash and green (unripe) tomatoes.

When choosing dried fruit for pickling, select the fully dried type, rather than the softer ready-to-eat variety that is popular for general cooking. The former has a better texture when soaked for a long time in pickling vinegar.

HOW TO MAKE CHUTNEYS

These are made from finely cut ingredients, cooked slowly with vinegar, a sweetener and frequently spices or other flavourings to make a thick, savoury jam-like mixture. Onions and apples are often included in chutneys, but almost any fruits and vegetables can be used. Chutneys should be matured in a cool dark place for at least 2 months before eating.

making tomato chutney

Makes about 2.25kg/5lb

INGREDIENTS

450g/1lb onions, chopped

900ml/1½ pints/3¾ cups malt vinegar

50g/2oz whole pickling spices, such as peppercorns, allspice berries, dried chillies, dried ginger and celery seeds

1kg/2¼lb ripe tomatoes, skinned and chopped

450g/1lb cooking apples, peeled, cored and chopped

350g/12oz/1½ cups soft light brown sugar

10ml/2 tsp salt

225g/8oz/1 cup sultanas (golden raisins)

1 Put the onions and vinegar in a large pan. Tie the pickling spices in a muslin (cheesecloth) bag and add to the pan. Bring slowly to the boil, then simmer gently for 30 minutes until the onions are almost tender.

2 Add the tomatoes and apples to the pan, and simmer for 10 minutes until the fruit is softened and starts to break down slightly.

3 Add the sugar and salt to the pan, and stir over a low heat until the sugar has dissolved completely, then stir in the sultanas.

4 Gently simmer the chutney for 1½–2 hours, stirring occasionally to prevent the mixture sticking. The chutney is ready when it is thick and there is no liquid on the surface. Draw a wooden spoon across the base of the pan: it should leave a clear line in the mixture.

5 Remove the pan from the heat and leave to cool for 5 minutes. Remove the spice bag and discard. Stir the mixture to ensure the chutney is evenly mixed, then spoon into warmed, sterilized jars.

6 Use the handle of a wooden spoon to release any trapped air bubbles and ensure the chutney is packed down well. Seal the jars immediately and leave to cool. Store the chutney in a cool, dark place and leave to mature for at least 1 month before eating. Use within 2 years.

TIPS FOR SUCCESSFUL CHUTNEY-MAKING

• Use malt vinegar for its intense flavour. Wine vinegar or cider vinegar are better for preserving colourful or light-coloured vegetables because they will not spoil the colour of the vegetables.

• The choice of sugar will affect the end result: brown sugar gives the richest flavour and colour; demerara (raw) sugar and golden granulated sugar give a caramel flavour; and white sugar helps to retain the colour of light ingredients.

• Never cover the pan when making chutney. Cooking the preserve uncovered allows the liquid to evaporate and the chutney to thicken. Towards the end, stir the chutney frequently to prevent it from catching and burning on the base of the pan.

• Always store chutney in a cool dark place: warmth can cause it to ferment, and bright sunlight can affect the colour.

HOW TO MAKE RELISHES

These are similar to chutneys, but are cooked for a shorter length of time to give a crisper, fresher result. The fruits and vegetables are usually cut into slightly smaller, neater pieces, and wine or cider vinegar is more frequently used than malt vinegar. Relishes contain a low proportion of vinegar and sugar, so do not keep for long. They can be eaten immediately or chilled and used within 2–3 months.

making hot pepper relish

Makes about 1.3kg/3lb

INGREDIENTS

900g/2lb red (bell) peppers, quartered, cored and seeded

10ml/2 tsp salt

4 fresh red chillies, seeded

450g/1lb red (Italian) onions, finely chopped

400ml/14fl oz/1⅔ cups red wine vinegar

5ml/1 tsp celery seeds

6 black peppercorns

200g/7oz/1 cup granulated sugar

1 Cut the peppers into 1cm/½in pieces and layer them in a colander or sieve placed over a large bowl, sprinkling salt between each layer. Leave the peppers to drain for at least 30 minutes.

2 Tip the red peppers into a large heavy pan and add the chillies, onions and vinegar.

3 Tie the celery seeds and black peppercorns in a square of muslin (cheesecloth) and add to the pan. Slowly bring to the boil over a low heat. Reduce the heat and simmer for about 25 minutes, or until the peppers are just tender.

4 Add the sugar and stir over a low heat until dissolved. Bring to the boil and simmer for 15 minutes, or until the relish is thick.

5 Remove the spice bag from the pan and discard. Spoon the relish into warmed, sterilized jars and seal. Store in the refrigerator and use within 3 months.

RELISHES WITH THICKENED SAUCES

Some relishes have a sauce base thickened with flour or cornflour (cornstarch). Mustard or turmeric may be added to the relish to give it a yellow colour. Corn relish, piccalilli and chow-chow are examples. The vegetables should retain their shape and be slightly crunchy, rather than soft.

making mustard relish

Makes about 1.3kg/3lb

INGREDIENTS

900g/2lb mixed vegetables, such as cauliflower, green beans, courgettes (zucchini), carrots, (bell) peppers and green tomatoes

225g/8oz shallots, finely sliced

750ml/1¼ pints/3 cups malt vinegar

1 garlic clove, crushed

50g/2oz/½ cup plain (all-purpose) flour

25g/1oz/¼ cup English mustard powder

200g/7oz/1 cup caster (superfine) sugar

2.5ml/½ tsp ground coriander

5ml/1 tsp salt

1 Break the cauliflower into small florets, cut the beans into 2.5cm/1in lengths and dice the courgettes, carrots, peppers and tomatoes.

2 Put the shallots in a large heavy pan with 600ml/1 pint/2½ cups of the vinegar. Simmer, uncovered, for 10 minutes. Add the vegetables and garlic and simmer for 10 minutes.

3 Mix together the flour, mustard, sugar, coriander, salt and remaining vinegar to make a smooth paste, then stir into the vegetables. Simmer for 10 minutes, stirring. Pot and store for 2 weeks before eating. Use within 6 months.

HOW TO MAKE SAVOURY JELLIES

MAKING JELLIES

Jellies are made using the juice which has been strained from simmered fruit, which is then boiled with sugar to setting point. The fruit requires very little preparation, other than giving it a rinse under the tap and roughly chopping larger fruit, but you do need to allow plenty of time to make the jelly itself. The secret to making a beautifully clear jelly lies in straining the fruit pulp through a jelly bag, which often takes several hours.

Jelly-making requires three substances – pectin, sugar and acid – in order for the jelly to set properly. A perfectly set jelly should retain its shape and quiver when spooned out of the jar. Fruits that are low in pectin such as strawberries, cherries and pears are not suitable on their own for making jellies, so they are usually combined with high-pectin fruit.

Because the fruit pulp is discarded in jelly-making, the yield is usually not very high. For this reason many jelly recipes use wild fruits, or gluts of home-grown fruit.

Jellies can be served both as sweet and savoury preserves. Some, such as redcurrant, rowan and cranberry jellies, are classic accompaniments for hot or cold roasted meat or game, or are added to gravy for flavour and to give an attractive glossy finish. Savoury jellies often contain chopped herbs and sometimes wine vinegar or cider vinegar to give it a sharper flavour.

yield of jelly

The final yield of jelly depends on how juicy the fruit is, and this can vary depending on the time of the year, the weather during growth and its ripeness when harvested. Because of this, the juice, rather than the fruit, is measured, and the amount of sugar is calculated accordingly. As a general rule, 450g/1lb/2¼ cups sugar is added for each 600ml /1 pint/2½ cups juice, although this may be less if the fruit is very rich in pectin. As a rough guide, recipes containing 450g/1lb/ 2¼ cups sugar will make about 675–800g/1½–1¾lb jelly.

making redcurrant jelly

Makes about 1.3kg/3lb

INGREDIENTS

1.3kg/3lb just-ripe redcurrants

600ml/1 pint/2½ cups water

about 900g/2lb/4½ cups preserving
  or granulated sugar

1 Check the fruit is clean. If necessary, rinse in cold water and use a little less water in the recipe.

2 Remove the currants from the stalks. There is no need to top and tail the fruit.

3 Place the redcurrants in a large heavy pan with the water and simmer gently for about 30 minutes, or until the fruit is soft. Stir occasionally.

4 Pour the cooked fruit and juices into a sterilized jelly bag suspended over a large bowl. Leave to drain for about 4 hours, or until the juice stops dripping. (Do not press or squeeze the fruit in the bag because this will result in a cloudy jelly.)

5 Discard the pulp remaining in the bag (unless you plan to boil the pulp a second time – see page 31). Pour the juice into the cleaned pan and add 450g/1lb/2¼ cups warmed sugar for each 600ml/1 pint/2½ cups of juice. (When making jellies with low-pectin fruit or vegetables, stir in a little lemon juice or vinegar to improve the set. This will also help to offset the sweetness of the jelly.)

6 Heat the mixture gently, stirring frequently, until the sugar has completely dissolved, then increase the heat and bring to the boil.

7 Boil the jelly rapidly for about 10 minutes, or until setting point is reached. You can check this using the flake or wrinkle test, or you can use a sugar thermometer. The jelly should be heated to 105°C/220°F.

8 Remove the pan from the heat, then skim any froth from the surface of the jelly using a slotted spoon.

9 Carefully remove the last traces of froth using a piece of kitchen paper. Pot the jelly immediately because it will start to set fairly quickly.

10 Cover and seal the jelly while it is hot, then leave to cool completely. (Do not move or tilt the jars until the jelly is completely cold and set.) Label the jars and store in a cool, dark place.

USING A JELLY BAG

Jelly bags, which are made from heavy-duty calico, cotton flannel or close-weave nylon, allow only the juice from the fruit to flow through, leaving the skins, pulp and pips (seeds) inside the bag. The fruit pulp and juices are very heavy, so strong tape or loops are positioned on the corners for hanging the bag securely on a stand, upturned stool or chair.

1 Before use, sterilize the jelly bag by scalding in boiling water. This process also helps the juices to run through the bag, rather than being absorbed into it.

2 If you don't have a jelly bag, you can use three or four layers of sterilized muslin (cheesecloth) or a piece of fine linen cloth instead. Simply line a large nylon or stainless-steel sieve with the muslin or linen.

3 Carefully suspend the jelly bag or lined sieve over a large bowl to catch the juice. Make sure the bag or sieve is secure before spooning some of the simmered fruit and juices into it. (Don't add too much to start with.)

4 Leave the fruit to drain for a while, then spoon in more fruit. Continue gradually adding fruit in this way until it has all been placed in the bag or sieve, then leave to drain until it stops dripping completely. Some fruits will take 2–3 hours to release all their juice, while others may take as long as 12 hours.

5 Immediately after use, wash the jelly bag thoroughly, then rinse several times to remove all traces of detergent. Ensure the bag is completely dry before storing. The jelly bag may be reused many times, but be sure to sterilize it before every use.

boiling fruit twice

Rather than discarding the fruit pulp from the jelly bag after draining, you can boil it again to extract more liquid and flavour. This should be done only with pectin-rich fruits such as sharp apples, damsons or currants. The resulting jelly may have a slightly less concentrated flavour than jelly made from juice obtained from fruit that has been boiled once.

To boil the fruit a second time, return the fruit pulp to the pan and add just enough cold water to cover, using no more than half the amount of water used for the first boiling. Simmer the fruit gently for about 20 minutes, then drain through the jelly bag as before. Add the juice to the first batch.

flavouring jelly

Savoury jellies are often flavoured with fresh herbs such as thyme, mint, sage and rosemary. In some, such as mint jelly, the herb is most important and the fruit provides a base in which to suspend the herb; in others, herbs are used in small quantities to impart a subtle flavour.

1 To simply add flavour, add sprigs of herbs at the beginning of cooking. Woody herbs should be removed before draining because stems may damage the jelly bag.

2 When adding finely chopped herbs to the finished jelly, even distribution can be difficult and, if the jelly is too hot, the pieces may float to the top. To overcome this problem, put the herbs in a sieve and sprinkle with a little water to dampen them.

3 Leave the jelly to stand until it just starts to form a thin skin on top, then quickly stir in the chopped herbs. Pot straight away in very warm, but not hot, sterilized jars and seal. Cool before labelling.

4 Herb sprigs and aromatic leaves, such as lemon verbena or geranium leaves, can look stunning set in jelly. Pour the jelly into sterilized jars, then leave until semi-set and insert the herb sprigs or leaves.

TIPS FOR SUCCESSFUL JELLY-MAKING

• There is no need to peel or stone (pit) fruit before cooking because all the debris will be removed during straining. However, it is important to discard any bruised or mouldy parts of the fruit because these will spoil the flavour. Rinse the fruit only if dusty or dirty.

• If using fruits such as apples that require longer cooking, chop the fruit very finely to reduce the cooking time required. Cooking the fruit for a shorter time also helps to give the jelly an intense, fresh flavour.

• Simmer the fruit very gently to extract the maximum amount of pectin and to avoid evaporating too much liquid. When cooking hard fruits that take a long time to soften, cover the pan for the first half of the cooking time to reduce the amount of liquid lost.

• Some fruits such as redcurrants or blackcurrants can be cooked in the oven to make highly flavoured jellies. Place the fruit in an oven-proof dish with about 75ml/5 tbsp water, cover tightly and cook at 140°C/275°F/Gas 1 for about 50 minutes, stirring occasionally, until pulpy. Drain through a jelly bag, then add 125g/15oz/generous 2 cups sugar for every 600ml/1 pint/2½ cups strained juice.

• Jellies set very quickly, so pot immediately. Warm a stainless steel funnel in the oven, or rinse a plastic one under hot water and dry it, then use to pot the jelly. If the jelly starts to set in the pan, warm it briefly until liquid again.

• Gently tap the jars as you fill with jelly to remove air bubbles.

• Although you can add a little butter to jam to disperse any scum, do not do this with jelly – it will make it cloudy.

HOW TO MAKE SALSAS

These fresh sauces and relishes originated in Mexico. They are made from fresh raw fruit and vegetables and usually flavoured with spices such as chilli and aromatic herbs such as coriander (cilantro). They may be hot and fiery or cool and refreshing.

Many salsas are meant to be eaten on the day of making. Some, however, are lightly cooked and will keep for a short time in the refrigerator. They can also be frozen and stored in the freezer for up to 2 months.

Vinegar and sugar may be included in salsas, but only as flavouring ingredients and not as preservatives. Like relishes, they are ready for eating immediately.

making sweet pepper and tomato salsa

This light and refreshing salsa uses similar ingredients to a relish, but the result is completely different due to the very short cooking time.

Makes about 900g/2lb

INGREDIENTS

450g/1lb firm ripe tomatoes

7.5ml/1½ tsp salt

675g/1½lb red, yellow and green (bell) peppers, quartered and seeded

1 onion

2 large fresh green chillies, seeded

1 garlic clove, crushed

45ml/3 tbsp olive oil

30ml/2 tbsp red wine vinegar

5ml/1 tsp caster (superfine) sugar

30ml/2 tbsp chopped fresh coriander (cilantro)

1 Cut a small cross in the base of each tomato and place in a large, heatproof bowl. Pour over boiling water to cover, then leave to stand for about 30 seconds. Drain the tomatoes and peel off the skins.

2 Cut the tomatoes into quarters and use a teaspoon to scoop out the seeds. (This gives a more attractive result and prevents the salsa becoming too wet.)

3 Cut the tomato flesh into 5mm/¼in pieces and layer them up in a nylon or stainless-steel sieve set over a bowl, sprinkling a little salt between each layer. Leave to drain for about 20 minutes.

4 Meanwhile, cut the peppers and onion into 5mm/¼in pieces and finely slice the chillies, ensuring all the white membrane has been discarded. Put in a large pan.

5 Add the chopped tomatoes to the pan and add the crushed garlic, olive oil, vinegar, sugar and fresh coriander. Bring the mixture to the boil and simmer for 5 minutes, stirring frequently.

6 If you are going to use the salsa quickly, spoon into clean jars, packing it down well, then seal. Store in the refrigerator and use within 2–3 days.

7 Alternatively, pack the salsa into freezerproof containers and freeze for up to 2 months. Before serving, remove the salsa from the freezer and place in the refrigerator. Leave to defrost overnight.

COOK'S TIPS

• It is important to lightly cook all the ingredients, including the coriander, because this kills enzymes that would otherwise cause the salsa to deteriorate more quickly.

• The oily substance, capsaicin, which is found in chillies, can cause intense irritation to the skin and eyes. Always wash your hands with soap and water immediately after handling chillies. Alternatively, protect your hands by wearing a pair of rubber (latex) gloves when chopping the chillies.

HOW TO MAKE SAUCES

Made with similar ingredients to chutneys, sauces have a thinner consistency and are sieved to a smooth purée. Those made with vegetables low in acid must either be stored in the refrigerator and consumed quickly, or heat-treated.

making tomato ketchup

Makes about 600ml/1 pint/2½ cups

INGREDIENTS

900g/2lb ripe tomatoes
225g/8oz shallots, peeled
2cm/¾in piece fresh root ginger, peeled
2 garlic cloves, peeled
150ml/¼ pint/⅔ cup cider vinegar
about 40g/1½oz/scant ¼ cup granulated
  or soft light brown sugar
5ml/1 tsp paprika
5ml/1 tsp salt

1 Roughly chop the tomatoes, shallots, ginger and garlic. Make the pieces fairly small, so that the mixture cooks quickly and retains its fresh flavour.

2 Put the chopped vegetables in a large heavy pan and slowly bring to the boil, stirring frequently until the juices start to run. Reduce the heat, cover and simmer for about 20 minutes, stirring frequently, until the shallots are tender.

3 Spoon the tomato mixture into a sieve placed over a clean pan and press through using the back of a spoon. Alternatively, push the mixture through a food mill.

4 Bring the tomato purée to the boil, then reduce the heat and simmer gently for 45 minutes, or until reduced by half.

5 Add the vinegar, sugar, paprika and salt to the pan and stir to combine. Simmer the sauce for a further 45 minutes, stirring frequently, until well reduced and thickened. (The hot sauce should be a slightly thinner consistency at this stage than is required for the final ketchup; it will thicken as it cools.)

6 Using a funnel, carefully pour the hot sauce into hot sterilized bottles, then seal with corks and heat-treat. (If the bottles are not going to be heat-treated, plastic screw caps can be used instead of corks.)

7 Store the ketchup in a cool dark place, preferably the refrigerator. If it has been heat-treated, it will keep for up to 2 years; if it has simply been bottled, it will keep for up to 2 months in the refrigerator.

HEAT-TREATING BOTTLES

Bottles must have a ridge on the neck, so that the cork can be secured with string.

1 Press a cork into the neck of a filled bottle and make a shallow cut across the top of the cork. Cut a 40cm/16in length of string. Keeping one end about 20cm/8in longer than the other, wedge the string into the cut.

2 Loop the longest end of string around the bottle neck, then pull the end through the front of the loop. Pull both ends down to tighten. Securely tie the loose ends of the string on the top of the cork. Repeat with the other bottles.

3 Wrap cloth around each bottle, then stand on a thick layer of cloth in a deep pan. Pour water up to the bottle necks and heat for 20 minutes for 600ml/1 pint/2½ cup hot-packed bottles; 25 minutes for 1 litre/1¾ pint/4 cup hot-packed and 600ml/1 pint/2½ cup cold-packed bottles; and 30 minutes for 1 litre/1¾ pint/4 cup cold-packed bottles.

pickles

Sharp and sweet, warm and mellow, or hot and piquant – pickles are the magical condiments that can transform simple foods into exhilarating meals. Fresh fruits and vegetables preserved in salt or vinegar and flavoured with spices and herbs make fabulously tasty and aromatic accompaniments to cold meats and cheeses, and go well with many roast meats too. They are simple to make and gloriously varied – each one with its own unique character and taste.

dill pickles

Redolent of garlic and piquant with fresh chilli, salty dill pickles can be supple and succulent or crisp and crunchy. Every pickle aficionado has a favourite type.

Makes about 900g/2lb

INGREDIENTS

20 small, ridged or knobbly pickling (small) cucumbers
2 litres/3½ pints/8 cups water
175g/6oz/¾ cup coarse sea salt
15–20 garlic cloves, unpeeled
2 bunches fresh dill
15ml/1 tbsp dill seeds
30ml/2 tbsp mixed pickling spice
1 or 2 hot fresh chillies

1 Scrub the cucumbers and rinse well in cold water. Leave to dry.

2 Put the measured water and salt in a large pan and bring to the boil. Turn off the heat and leave to cool to room temperature.

3 Using the flat side of a knife blade or a wooden mallet, lightly crush each garlic clove, breaking the papery skin.

4 Pack the cucumbers tightly into one or two wide-necked, sterilized jars, layering them with the garlic, fresh dill, dill seeds and pickling spice. Add one chilli to each jar. Pour over the cooled brine, making sure that the cucumbers are completely covered. Tap the jars on the work surface to dispel any trapped air bubbles.

5 Cover the jars with lids and then leave to stand at room temperature for 4–7 days before serving. Store in the refrigerator.

COOK'S TIP

If you cannot find ridged or knobbly pickling cucumbers, use any kind of small cucumbers instead.

pickled mushrooms with garlic

This method of preserving mushrooms is popular throughout Europe. The pickle is good made with cultivated mushrooms, but it is worth including a couple of sliced ceps for their flavour.

Makes about 900g/2lb

INGREDIENTS

500g/1¼lb/8 cups mixed mushrooms, such as small ceps, chestnut mushrooms, shiitake and girolles

300ml/½ pint/1¼ cups white wine vinegar or cider vinegar

15ml/1 tbsp sea salt

5ml/1 tsp caster (superfine) sugar

300ml/½ pint/1¼ cups water

4–5 fresh bay leaves

8 large fresh thyme sprigs

15 garlic cloves, peeled, halved, with any green shoots removed

1 small red onion, halved and thinly sliced

2–3 small dried red chillies

5ml/1 tsp coriander seeds, lightly crushed

5ml/1 tsp black peppercorns

a few strips of lemon rind

250–350ml/8–12fl oz/1–1½ cups extra virgin olive oil

1 Trim and wipe the mushrooms and cut any large ones in half.

2 Put the vinegar, salt, sugar and water in a pan and bring to the boil. Add the bay leaves, thyme, garlic, onion, chillies, coriander seeds, peppercorns and lemon rind and simmer for 2 minutes.

3 Add the mushrooms to the pan and simmer for 3–4 minutes. Drain the mushrooms through a seive, retaining all the herbs and spices, then set aside for a few minutes more until the mushrooms are thoroughly drained.

4 Fill one large or two small cool sterilized jars with the mushrooms. Distribute the garlic, onion, herbs and spices evenly among the layers of mushrooms, then add enough olive oil to cover by at least 1cm/½in. You may need to use extra oil if you are making two jars.

5 Leave the pickle to settle, then tap the jars on the work surface to dispel any air bubbles. Seal the jars, then store in the refrigerator. Use within 2 weeks.

pickled red cabbage

This delicately spiced and vibrant-coloured pickle is an old-fashioned favourite to serve with bread and cheese for an informal lunch, or to use to accompany cold ham, duck or goose.

Makes about 1–1.6kg/2¼–3½lb

INGREDIENTS

675g/1½lb/6 cups red cabbage, shredded

1 large Spanish onion, sliced

30ml/2 tbsp sea salt

600ml/1 pint/2½ cups red wine vinegar

75g/3oz/6 tbsp light muscovado (brown) sugar

15ml/1 tbsp coriander seeds

3 cloves

2.5cm/1in piece fresh root ginger

1 whole star anise

2 bay leaves

4 eating apples

1 Put the cabbage and onion in a bowl, add the salt and mix well until thoroughly combined. Tip the mixture into a colander over a bowl and leave to drain overnight.

2 The next day, rinse the salted vegetables, drain well and pat dry using kitchen paper.

3 Pour the vinegar into a pan, add the sugar, spices and bay leaves and bring to the boil. Remove from the heat and leave to cool.

4 Core and chop the apples, then layer with the cabbage and onions in sterilized preserving jars. Pour over the cooled spiced vinegar. (If you prefer a milder pickle, strain out the spices first.) Seal the jars and store for 1 week before eating. Eat within 2 months. Once opened, store in the refrigerator.

pickled turnips and beetroot

This delicious pickle is a Middle Eastern speciality. The turnips turn a rich red in their beetroot-spiked brine and look gorgeous stacked on shelves in the store cupboard.

2 Put the salt and water in a bowl, stir and leave to stand until the salt has completely dissolved.

3 Sprinkle the beetroot with lemon juice and place in the bottom of four 1.2 litre/2 pint sterilized jars. Top with sliced turnip, packing them in very tightly, then pour over the brine, making sure that the vegetables are covered.

4 Seal the jars and leave in a cool place for 7 days before serving.

Makes about 1.6kg/3½lb

INGREDIENTS
1kg/2¼lb young turnips
3–4 raw beetroot (beets)
about 45ml/3 tbsp coarse sea salt
about 1.5 litres/2½ pints/6¼ cups water
juice of 1 lemon

COOK'S TIP
Be careful when preparing the beetroot because their bright red juice can stain clothing.

1 Wash the turnips and beetroot, but do not peel them, then cut into slices about 5mm/¼in thick.

shallots in balsamic vinegar

These whole shallots, cooked in balsamic vinegar and herbs, are a modern variation on traditional pickled onions. They have a much more gentle, smooth flavour and are delicious served with cold meats or robustly flavoured hard cheeses.

Makes one large jar

INGREDIENTS

500g/1¼lb shallots

30ml/2 tbsp muscovado (molasses) sugar

several bay leaves and/or fresh thyme sprigs

300ml/½ pint/1¼ cups balsamic vinegar

VARIATION

Use other robust herbs in place of the thyme sprigs. Rosemary, oregano or marjoram are all good choices.

1 Put the unpeeled shallots in a bowl. Pour over boiling water and leave to stand for 2 minutes to loosen the skins. Drain and peel the shallots, leaving them whole.

2 Put the sugar, bay leaves and/or thyme and vinegar in a large heavy pan and bring to the boil. Add the shallots, cover and simmer gently for about 40 minutes, or until the shallots are just tender.

3 Transfer the shallots and vinegar mixture to a warmed sterilized jar, packing the shallots down well. Seal and label the jar, then store in a cool, dark place for about 1 month before eating.

hot thai pickled shallots

Although they may be quite difficult to find and require lengthy preparation, Thai pink shallots look and taste exquisite in this spiced pickle. The shallots taste good finely sliced, and served as a condiment with a wide range of South-east Asian meals.

Makes about three jars

INGREDIENTS

5–6 fresh red or green bird's eye chillies, halved and seeded if liked

500g/1¼lb Thai pink shallots, peeled

2 large garlic cloves, peeled, halved and green shoots removed

600ml/1 pint/2½ cups cider vinegar

45ml/3 tbsp granulated sugar

10ml/2 tsp salt

5cm/2in piece fresh root ginger, sliced

15ml/1 tbsp coriander seeds

2 lemon grass stalks, cut in half lengthways

4 kaffir lime leaves or strips of lime rind

15ml/1 tbsp chopped fresh coriander (cilantro)

1 If leaving the chillies whole (they will be hotter), prick several times with a cocktail stick (toothpick).

2 Bring a large pan of water to the boil. Blanch the chillies, shallots and garlic for 1–2 minutes, then drain. Rinse the vegetables under cold water and leave to drain.

VARIATION

Ordinary shallots and pickling onions are widely available and can be preserved using the same method.

3 To prepare the vinegar, put the cider vinegar, sugar, salt, ginger, coriander seeds, lemon grass and lime leaves or lime rind in a large pan and bring to the boil. Simmer over a low heat for 3–4 minutes, then remove from the heat and set aside to cool.

4 Using a slotted spoon, remove the sliced ginger from the pan and discard. Return the vinegar to the boil, then add the fresh coriander, garlic and chillies, and cook for about 1 minute.

5 Pack the shallots, spices and aromatics into warmed sterilized jars and pour over the hot vinegar. Cool, then seal. Leave in a dark place for 2 months before eating.

english pickled onions

These powerful pickles are traditionally served with a plate of cold meats and bread and cheese. They should be made with malt vinegar and stored for at least 6 weeks before eating.

Makes about four jars

INGREDIENTS

1kg/2¼lb pickling onions
115g/4oz/½ cup salt
750ml/1¼ pints/3 cups malt vinegar
15ml/1 tbsp sugar
2–3 dried red chillies
5ml/1 tsp brown mustard seeds
15ml/1 tbsp coriander seeds
5ml/1 tsp allspice berries
5ml/1 tsp black peppercorns
5cm/2in piece fresh root ginger, sliced
2–3 blades mace
2–3 fresh bay leaves

1 To peel the onions, trim off the root ends, but leave the onion layers attached. Cut a thin slice off the top (neck) end of the onion. Place the onions in a bowl, then cover with boiling water. Leave to stand for about 4 minutes, then drain. The skin should then be easy to peel using a small, sharp knife.

2 Place the peeled onions in a bowl and cover with cold water, then drain the water into a large pan. Add the salt and heat slightly to dissolve it, then cool before pouring the brine over the onions.

3 Place a plate inside the top of the bowl and weigh it down slightly so that it keeps all the onions submerged in the brine. Leave to stand for 24 hours.

4 Meanwhile, place the vinegar in a large pan. Wrap all the remaining ingredients, except the bay leaves, in a piece of muslin (cheesecloth). Bring to the boil, simmer for about 5 minutes, then remove the pan from the heat. Set aside and leave to infuse overnight.

5 The next day, drain the onions, rinse and pat dry. Pack them into sterilized 450g/1lb jars. Add some or all of the spice from the vinegar, except the ginger slices. The pickle will become hotter if you add the chillies. Pour the vinegar over to cover and add the bay leaves. (Store leftover vinegar in a bottle for another batch of pickles.)

6 Seal the jars with non-metallic lids and store in a cool, dark place for at least 6 weeks before eating.

instant pickle of mixed vegetables

This fresh, salad-style pickle doesn't need lengthy storing so makes the perfect choice if you need a bowl of pickle immediately. However, it does not have good storing properties.

Makes about 450g/1lb

INGREDIENTS

½ cauliflower head, cut into florets

2 carrots, sliced

2 celery sticks, thinly sliced

¼–½ white cabbage, thinly sliced

115g/4oz/scant 1 cup runner (green) beans, cut into bitesize pieces

6 garlic cloves, sliced

1–4 fresh chillies, whole or sliced

5cm/2in piece fresh root ginger, sliced

1 red (bell) pepper, sliced

2.5ml/½ tsp turmeric

105ml/7 tbsp white wine vinegar

15–30ml/1–2 tbsp granulated sugar

60–90ml/4–6 tbsp olive oil

juice of 2 lemons

salt

1 Toss the cauliflower, carrots, celery, cabbage, beans, garlic, chillies, ginger and pepper with salt and leave them to stand in a colander over a bowl for 4 hours.

2 Shake the vegetables well to remove any excess juices.

3 Transfer the salted vegetables to a bowl. Add the turmeric, vinegar, sugar to taste, oil and lemon juice. Toss to combine, then add enough water to distribute the flavours. Cover the bowl and leave to chill for at least 1 hour, or until you are ready to serve.

stuffed baby aubergines

This Middle Eastern fermented pickle makes a succulent and spicy accompaniment to cold meats, but is equally good served with a few salad leaves and bread as a simple appetizer.

Makes about 3 jars

INGREDIENTS

1kg/2¼lb baby aubergines (eggplant)
2 fresh red chillies, halved lengthways
2 green chillies, halved lengthways
2 celery sticks, cut into matchstick strips
2 carrots, cut into matchstick strips
4 garlic cloves, peeled and finely chopped
20ml/4 tsp salt
4 small fresh vine leaves (optional)
750ml/1¼ pints/3 cups cooled boiled water
45ml/3 tbsp white wine vinegar

1 Trim the aubergine stems, but do not remove them completely. Cut a slit lengthways along each aubergine, almost through to the other side, to make a pocket.

COOK'S TIPS

• Aubergines come in a multitude of colours from a deep purple-black to yellow and creamy white. Whichever type you use, choose ones with taut, glossy skins.
• Steam the aubergines as soon as you have slit them open because their flesh discolours rapidly when exposed to air.

2 Steam the slit aubergines for 5–6 minutes or until they are just tender when tested with the tip of a sharp knife.

3 Put the aubergines in a colander set over a bowl, then place a plate on top. Place a few weights on the plate to press it down gently and leave for 4 hours to squeeze out the moisture from the vegetables.

4 Finely chop two red and two green chilli halves and place in a bowl. Add the celery and carrots to the chillies with the garlic and 5ml/1 tsp of the salt. Mix and use to stuff the aubergine pockets.

5 Tightly pack the aubergines, remaining chillies and vine leaves, if using, into a large sterilized jar.

6 Pour the water into a jug (pitcher) and add the remaining 15ml/1 tbsp salt and the vinegar. Stir together until the salt has dissolved. Pour enough brine into the jar to cover the aubergines, then weigh down the top.

7 Cover the jar with a clean dishtowel and leave in a warm, well-ventilated place to ferment. The brine will turn cloudy as fermentation starts, but will clear after 1–2 weeks when the pickle has finished fermenting. As soon as this happens, cover and seal the jar and store in the refrigerator. Eat the pickle within 2 months.

preserved lemons

These richly flavoured fruits are widely used in Middle Eastern cooking. Only the rind, which contains the essential flavour of the lemon is used in recipes. Traditionally whole lemons are preserved, but this recipe uses wedges, which can be packed into jars more easily.

2 Pack the salted lemon wedges into two 1.2 litre/2 pint/5 cup warmed sterilized jars. To each jar, add 30–45ml/2–3 tbsp sea salt and half the lemon juice, then top up with boiling water to cover the lemon wedges. Seal the jars and leave to stand for 2–4 weeks before using.

3 To use, rinse the preserved lemons well to remove some of the salty flavour, then pull off and discard the flesh. Cut the lemon rind into strips or leave in chunks and use as desired.

Makes about 2 jars

INGREDIENTS

10 unwaxed lemons

about 200ml/7fl oz/scant 1 cup fresh lemon juice or a combination of fresh and preserved juice

boiling water

sea salt

COOK'S TIP

The salty, well-flavoured juice that is used to preserve the lemons can be used to flavour salad dressings or added to hot sauces.

1 Wash the lemons well and cut each into six to eight wedges. Press a generous amount of salt on to the cut surface of each wedge.

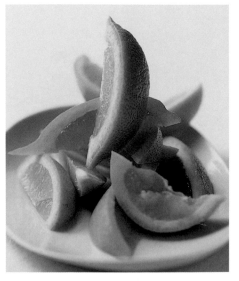

pickled limes

This hot, pungent pickle comes from the Punjab in India. Salting softens the rind and intensifies the flavour of the limes, while they mature in the first month or two of storage. Pickled limes are extremely salty so are best served with slightly under-seasoned dishes.

Makes about 1kg/2¼lb

INGREDIENTS

1kg/2¼lb unwaxed limes

75g/3oz/⅓ cup salt

seeds from 6 green cardamom pods

6 whole cloves

5ml/1 tsp cumin seeds

4 fresh red chillies, seeded
  and sliced

5cm/2in piece fresh root ginger, peeled
  and finely shredded

450g/1lb/2¼ cups preserving or
  granulated sugar

1 Put the limes in a large bowl and pour over cold water to cover. Leave to soak for 8 hours, or overnight, if preferred.

2 The next day, remove the limes from the water. Using a sharp knife, cut each lime in half from end to end, then cut each half into 5mm/¼in-thick slices.

3 Place the lime slices in the bowl, sprinkling the salt between the layers. Cover and leave to stand for a further 8 hours.

4 Drain the limes, catching the juices in a preserving pan. Crush the cardamom seeds with the cumin seeds. Add to the pan with the chillies, ginger and sugar. Bring to the boil, stirring until the sugar dissolves. Simmer for 2 minutes and leave to cool.

5 Mix the limes in the syrup. Pack into sterilized jars, cover and seal. Store in a cool, dark place for at least 1 month before eating. Use within 1 year.

striped spiced oranges

These delightful sweet-sour spiced orange slices have a wonderfully warming flavour and look very pretty. Serve them with baked ham, rich terrines and gamey pâtés. They are also delicious with roasted red peppers and grilled halloumi cheese.

Makes about 1.2kg/2½lb

INGREDIENTS

6 small or medium oranges

750ml/1¼ pints/3 cups white wine vinegar

900g/2lb/4½ cups preserving or granulated sugar

7.5cm/3in cinnamon stick

5ml/1 tsp whole allspice

8 whole cloves

45ml/3 tbsp brandy (optional)

COOK'S TIP

These preserved oranges, with their bright colour and warming flavour, make them a perfect accompaniment during the festive season – delicious with leftover turkey or wafer thin slices of festive ham.

1 Scrub the oranges well, then cut strips of rind from each one using a canelle knife (zester) to achieve a striped effect. Reserve the strips of rind.

2 Using a sharp knife, cut the oranges across into slices slightly thicker than 5mm/¼in. Remove and discard any pips (seeds).

3 Put the orange slices into a preserving pan and pour over just enough cold water to cover the fruit. Bring to the boil, then reduce the heat and simmer gently for about 5 minutes, or until the oranges are tender. Using a slotted spoon, transfer the orange slices to a large bowl and discard the cooking liquid.

4 Put the vinegar and sugar in the cleaned pan. Tie the cinnamon, whole allspice and orange rind together in muslin (cheesecloth) and add to the pan. Slowly bring to the boil, stirring, until the sugar has dissolved. Simmer for 1 minute.

5 Return the oranges slices to the pan and cook gently for about 30 minutes, or until the rind is translucent and the orange slices look glazed. Remove from the heat and discard the spice bag.

6 Using a slotted spoon, transfer the orange slices to hot sterilized jars, adding the cloves between the layers. Bring the syrup to a rapid boil and boil for about 10 minutes, or until slightly thickened.

7 Allow the syrup to cool for a few minutes, then stir in the brandy, if using. Pour the syrup into the jars, making sure that the fruit is completely immersed. Gently tap the jars on the work surface to release any air bubbles, then cover and seal. Store for at least 2 weeks before using. Use within 6 months.

pickled plums

This preserve is popular in Central Europe and works well for all varieties of plums, from small wild bullaces and astringent damsons to the more delicately flavoured yellow or red-flushed mirabelle. Plums soften easily, so make sure that you choose very firm fruit.

Makes about 900g/2lb

INGREDIENTS

900g/2lb firm plums

150ml/¼ pint/⅔ cup clear apple juice

450ml/¾ pint/scant 2 cups cider vinegar

2.5ml/½ tsp salt

8 allspice berries

2.5cm/1in piece fresh root ginger, peeled and cut into matchstick strips

4 bay leaves

675g/1½lb/scant 3½ cups preserving or granulated sugar

VARIATION

Juniper berries can be used instead of the allspice berries.

1 Wash the plums, then prick them once or twice using a wooden cocktail stick (toothpick). Put the apple juice, vinegar, salt, allspice berries, ginger and bay leaves in a preserving pan.

2 Add the plums to the pan and slowly bring to the boil. Reduce the heat and simmer gently for 10 minutes, or until the plums are just tender. Remove the plums with a slotted spoon and pack them into hot sterilized jars.

3 Add the sugar to the pan and stir over a low heat until dissolved. Boil steadily for 10 minutes, or until the mixture is syrupy.

4 Leave the syrup to cool for a few minutes, then pour over the plums. Cover and seal. Store for at least 1 month before using and use within 1 year of making.

italian mustard fruit pickles

This traditional and popular Italian preserve is made from late summer and autumn fruits, and then left to mature in time for Christmas when it is served with Italian steamed sausage. The fruits can be mixed together, or arranged in layers in the jars for a stunning effect.

Makes about 1.2kg/2½lb

INGREDIENTS

450ml/¾ pint/scant 2 cups white wine vinegar

30ml/2 tbsp mustard seeds

1kg/2¼lb mixed fruit, such as peaches, nectarines, apricots, plums, melon, figs and cherries

675g/1½lb/scant 3½ cups preserving or granulated sugar

VARIATION

If you prefer a slightly less tangy pickle, use cider vinegar instead of the white wine vinegar used here.

1 Put the vinegar and mustard seeds in a pan, bring to the boil, then simmer for 5 minutes. Remove from the heat, cover and leave to infuse for 1 hour. Strain the vinegar into a clean pan and discard the mustard seeds.

2 Prepare the fruit. Wash and pat dry the peaches, nectarines, apricots and plums, then stone (pit) and thickly slice or halve. Cut the melon in half, discard the seeds (pips), then slice into 1cm/½in pieces or scoop into balls using a melon baller. Cut the figs into quarters and remove the stalks from the cherries.

3 Add the sugar to the mustard vinegar and heat gently, stirring occasionally, until the sugar has dissolved completely. Bring to the boil, reduce the heat and simmer for 5 minutes, or until syrupy.

4 Add the fruit to the syrup and poach it over a gentle heat for 5–10 minutes. Some fruit will be ready sooner than others, so lift out as soon as each variety is tender, using a slotted spoon.

5 Pack the fruit into hot sterilized jars. Ladle the hot mustard syrup over the fruit. Cover and seal. Allow the pickles to mature for at least 1 month before eating. Use within 6 months.

sweet pickled watermelon rind

This unusual pickle has a slightly aromatic melon flavour and a crunchy texture. It's the perfect way to use up the part of the fruit that is normally discarded.

Makes about 900g/2lb

INGREDIENTS

900g/2lb watermelon rind
  (from 1 large fruit)

50g/2oz/¼ cup salt

900ml/1½ pints/3¾ cups water

450g/1lb/2¼ cups preserving or
  granulated sugar

300ml/½ pint/1¼ cups white wine vinegar

6 whole cloves

7.5cm/3in cinnamon stick

COOK'S TIP

Leave the watermelon rind to mature for at least 4 weeks before eating. This really helps the flavours to develop.

1 Remove the dark green skin from the watermelon rind, leaving a thin layer, no more than 3mm/⅛in thick, of the pink fruit. Cut the rind into slices about 5cm × 5mm/2 × ¼in thick, and place in a large bowl.

2 Dissolve the salt in 600ml/1 pint/2½ cups of the water. Pour over the watermelon rind, cover and leave for at least 6 hours or overnight.

3 Drain the watermelon rind and rinse under cold water. Put the rind in a pan and cover with fresh water. Bring the boil, reduce the heat and simmer for 10–15 minutes until just tender. Drain well.

4 Put the sugar, vinegar and remaining water in a clean pan. Tie the cloves and cinnamon in muslin (cheesecloth) and add to the pan. Heat gently, stirring occasionally, until the sugar has dissolved, then bring to the boil and simmer for 10 minutes. Turn off the heat. Add the rind, cover and leave to stand for about 2 hours.

5 Slowly bring the mixture back to the boil, then reduce the heat and simmer gently for 20 minutes, or until the rind has a translucent appearance. Remove and discard the spice bag. Place the rind in hot sterilized jars. Pour over the hot syrup, tapping the jar to release any trapped air. Cover and seal.

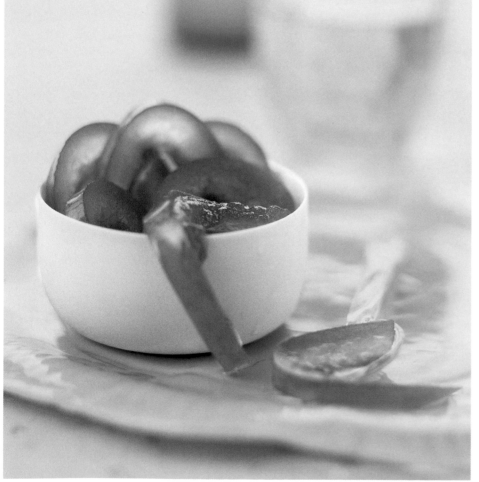

blushing pears

As this pickle matures, the fruits absorb the colour of the vinegar, giving them a glorious pink hue. They're especially good served with cold turkey, game pie, well-flavoured cheese or pâté.

Makes about 1.3kg/3lb

INGREDIENTS

1 small lemon

450g/1lb/2¼ cups golden granulated sugar

475ml/16fl oz/2 cups raspberry vinegar

7.5cm/3in cinnamon stick

6 whole cloves

6 allspice berries

150ml/¼ pint/⅔ cup water

900g/2lb firm pears

1 Using a sharp knife, thinly pare a few strips of rind from the lemon. Squeeze out 30ml/2 tbsp of the juice and put it in a large pan with the strips of rind.

2 Add the sugar, vinegar, spices and water to the pan. Heat gently, stirring occasionally, until the sugar has completely dissolved, then slowly bring to the boil.

VARIATION

Nectarines and peaches may be pickled using the same method. Blanch and skin the fruits, then halve and stone (pit). Add a strip of orange rind to the syrup instead of lemon rind.

3 Meanwhile, prepare the pears. Peel and halve the pears, then scoop out the cores using a melon baller or small teaspoon. If the pears are very large, cut them into quarters rather than halves.

4 Add the pears to the pan and simmer very gently for about 20 minutes, or until tender and translucent but still whole. Check the pears frequently towards the end of the cooking time. Using a slotted spoon, remove the pears from the pan and pack into hot sterilized jars, adding the spices and strips of lemon rind.

5 Boil the syrup for 5 minutes, or until slightly reduced. Skim off any scum, then ladle the syrup over the pears. Cover and seal. Store for at least 1 month before eating.

chutneys

Long, slow cooking produces the classic rich and intriguing flavours that epitomize thick, chunky chutneys. Fresh vegetables and fruits are combined with fresh herbs and spices, then simmered to perfection to created wonderfully mellow flavours. These versatile condiments are marvellous served with cold meats and cheeses, or spread thickly in sandwiches to enliven and enhance the simplest fillings.

green tomato chutney

This is a classic chutney for using the last tomatoes of summer that just never seem to ripen. Apples and onions contribute essential flavour, which is enhanced by the addition of spice.

Makes about 2.5kg/5½lb

INGREDIENTS

1.8kg/4lb green tomatoes, roughly chopped

450g/1lb cooking apples, peeled, cored and chopped

450g/1lb onions, chopped

2 large garlic cloves, crushed

15ml/1 tbsp salt

45ml/3 tbsp pickling spice

600ml/1 pint/2½ cups cider vinegar

450g/1lb/2¼ cups granulated sugar

COOK'S TIP

Allow the chutney to mature for at least 1 month before using.

1 Place the tomatoes, apples, onions and garlic in a large pan and add the salt.

2 Tie the pickling spice in a piece of muslin (cheesecloth) and add to the ingredients in the pan.

3 Add half the vinegar to the pan and bring to the boil. Reduce the heat and simmer for 1 hour, or until the chutney is reduced and thick, stirring frequently.

4 Put the sugar and remaining vinegar in a pan and heat gently until the sugar has dissolved, then add to the chutney. Simmer for 1½ hours until the chutney is thick, stirring it occasionally.

5 Remove the muslin bag from the chutney, then spoon the hot chutney into warmed sterilized jars. Cover and seal immediately.

COOK'S TIPS

• To avoid spillages and speed up the process of potting preserves, use a wide-necked jam funnel to transfer the chutney into the jars. Wipe the jars immediately, then label them when cold.

• Use a long-handled teaspoon to press and poke the chutney right down into the pots to exclude any trapped air pockets.

• Press wax discs on the surface of the chutney before sealing the jar.

tomato chutney

This spicy and dark, sweet-sour chutney is delicious served with a selection of well-flavoured cheeses and biscuits or bread, or with cold roast meats such as ham, turkey, tongue or lamb.

Makes about 1.8kg/4lb

INGREDIENTS

900g/2lb tomatoes, skinned

225g/8oz/1½ cups raisins

225g/8oz onions, chopped

225g/8oz/generous 1 cup caster (superfine) sugar

600ml/1 pint/2½ cups malt vinegar

VARIATION

Dried dates may be used in place of the raisins, and red wine or sherry vinegar may be used in place of the malt vinegar. Stone (pit) and chop the dates, or buy stoned cooking dates that have been compressed in a block and chop them finely.

1 Chop the tomatoes roughly and place in a preserving pan. Add the raisins, onions and caster sugar.

2 Pour the vinegar into the pan and bring the mixture to the boil. Simmer for 2 hours, uncovered, until soft and thickened.

3 Transfer the chutney to warmed sterilized jars. Top with waxed discs and lids. Store in a cool, dark place and leave to mature for 1 month. The chutney will keep unopened for up to 1 year. Once the jars have been opened, store them in the refrigerator.

mediterranean chutney

Reminiscent of the warm Mediterranean climate, this mixed vegetable chutney is colourful, mild and warm in flavour and goes particularly well with grilled meats and sausages. For a hotter, spicier flavour, add a little cayenne pepper with the paprika.

Makes about 1.8kg/4lb

INGREDIENTS

450g/1lb Spanish onions, chopped

900g/2lb ripe tomatoes, skinned and chopped

1 aubergine (eggplant), weighing about 350g/12oz, trimmed and cut into 1cm/½in cubes

450g/1lb courgettes (zucchini), sliced

1 yellow (bell) pepper, quartered, seeded and sliced

1 red (bell) pepper, quartered, seeded and sliced

3 garlic cloves, crushed

1 small sprig of rosemary

1 small sprig of thyme

2 bay leaves

15ml/1 tbsp salt

15ml/1 tbsp paprika

300ml/½ pint/1¼ cups malt vinegar

400g/14oz/2 cups granulated sugar

1 Put the chopped onions, tomatoes, aubergine, courgettes, peppers and garlic in a preserving pan. Cover the pan with a lid and cook gently over a very low heat, stirring occasionally, for about 15 minutes, or until the juices start to run.

2 Tie the rosemary, thyme and bay leaves in a piece of muslin (cheesecloth). Add to the pan with the salt, paprika and half the malt vinegar. Simmer, uncovered, for 25 minutes, or until the vegetables are tender and the juices reduced.

3 Add the remaining vinegar and sugar to the pan and stir over a low heat until the sugar has dissolved. Simmer for 30 minutes, stirring the chutney frequently towards the end of cooking time.

4 When the chutney is reduced to a thick consistency and no excess liquid remains, discard the herbs, then spoon the chutney into warmed sterilized jars. Set aside until cool, then cover and seal with vinegar-proof lids.

5 Store the chutney in a cool, dark place and allow to mature for at least 2 months before eating. Use the chutney within 2 years. Once opened, store in the refrigerator and use within 2 months.

confit of slow-cooked onions

This jam of slow-cooked, caramelized onions in sweet-sour balsamic vinegar will keep for several days in a sealed jar in the refrigerator. You can make it with red, white or yellow onions, but yellow onions will produce the sweetest result.

Makes about 500g/1¼lb

INGREDIENTS

30ml/2 tbsp olive oil

15g/½oz/1 tbsp butter

500g/1¼lb onions, sliced

3–5 fresh thyme sprigs

1 fresh bay leaf

30ml/2 tbsp light muscovado (brown) sugar, plus a little extra

50g/2oz/¼ cup ready-to-eat prunes, chopped

30ml/2 tbsp balsamic vinegar, plus a little extra

120ml/4fl oz/½ cup red wine

salt and ground black pepper

3 Add the prunes, vinegar, wine and 60ml/4 tbsp water to the pan and cook over a low heat, stirring frequently, for 20 minutes, or until most of the liquid has evaporated. Add a little more water and reduce the heat if it looks dry. Remove from the heat.

4 Adjust the seasoning if necessary, adding more sugar and/or vinegar to taste. Leave the confit to cool then stir in the remaining 5ml/ 1 tsp olive oil and serve.

VARIATION

Gently brown 500g/1¼lb peeled pickling (pearl) onions in 60ml/4 tbsp olive oil. Sprinkle in 45ml/3 tbsp brown sugar and caramelize a little, then add 7.5ml/1½ tsp crushed coriander seeds, 250ml/8fl oz/1 cup red wine, 2 bay leaves, a few thyme sprigs, 3 strips orange rind, 45ml/3 tbsp tomato purée (paste) and the juice of 1 orange. Cook gently, covered, for 1 hour, stirring occasionally. Uncover for the last 20 minutes. Sharpen with 15–30ml/ 1–2 tbsp sherry vinegar.

1 Reserve 5ml/1 tsp of the oil, then heat the remaining oil with the butter in a large pan. Add the onions, cover and cook gently over a low heat for about 15 minutes, stirring occasionally.

2 Season the onions with salt and ground black pepper, then add the thyme, bay leaf and sugar. Cook slowly, uncovered, for a further 15–20 minutes until the onions are very soft and dark. Stir the onions occasionally during cooking to prevent them sticking or burning.

kashmir chutney

In the true tradition of the Kashmiri country store, this is a typical family recipe passed down from generation to generation. It is wonderful served with plain or spicy grilled sausages.

Makes about 2.75kg/6lb

INGREDIENTS

1kg/2¼lb green eating apples
15g/½oz garlic cloves
1 litre/1¾ pints/4 cups malt vinegar
450g/1lb dates
115g/4oz preserved stem ginger
450g/1lb/3 cups raisins
450g/1lb/2 cups soft light brown sugar
2.5ml/½ tsp cayenne pepper
30ml/2 tbsp salt

COOK'S TIP

This sweet, chunky, spicy chutney is perfect served with cold meats for an informal buffet lunch.

1 Quarter the apples, remove the cores and chop coarsely. Peel and chop the garlic.

2 Place the apple and garlic in a pan with enough vinegar to cover. Bring to the boil and boil for 10 minutes.

3 Chop the dates and ginger and add them to the pan, together with the rest of the ingredients. Cook gently for 45 minutes.

4 Spoon the mixture into warmed sterilized jars and seal immediately.

fiery bengal chutney

Not for timid tastebuds, this fiery chutney is the perfect choice for lovers of hot and spicy food. Although it can be eaten a month after making, it is better matured for longer.

Makes about 2kg/4½lb

INGREDIENTS

115g/4oz fresh root ginger

1kg/2¼lb cooking apples

675g/1½lb onions

6 garlic cloves, finely chopped

225g/8oz/1½ cups raisins

450ml/¾ pint/scant 2 cups malt vinegar

400g/14oz/1¾ cups demerara (raw) sugar

2 fresh red chillies

2 fresh green chillies

15ml/1 tbsp salt

5ml/1 tsp turmeric

1 Peel and finely shred the fresh root ginger. Peel, core and roughly chop the apples. Peel and quarter the onions, then slice as thinly as possible. Place in a preserving pan with the garlic, raisins and vinegar.

2 Bring to the boil, then simmer steadily for 15–20 minutes, stirring occasionally, until the apples and onions are thoroughly softened. Add the sugar and stir over a low heat until the sugar has dissolved. Simmer the mixture for about 40 minutes, or until thick and pulpy, stirring frequently towards the end of the cooking time.

3 Halve the chillies and remove the seeds, then slice them finely. (Always wash your hands with soapy water immediately after handling chillies.)

4 Add the chillies to the pan and cook for a further 5–10 minutes, or until no excess liquid remains. Stir in the salt and turmeric.

5 Spoon the chutney into warmed sterilized jars, cover and seal them immediately, then label when cool.

6 Store the chutney in a cool, dark place and leave to mature for at least 2 months before eating. Use within 2 years of making. Once opened, store in the refrigerator and use within 1 month.

butternut, apricot and almond chutney

Coriander seeds and turmeric add a slightly spicy touch to this rich golden chutney. It is delicious in little canapés or with cubes of mozzarella cheese; it is also good in sandwiches.

Makes about 1.8kg/4lb

INGREDIENTS

1 small butternut squash, weighing about 800g/1¾lb

400g/14oz/2 cups golden granulated sugar

600ml/1 pint/2½ cups cider vinegar

2 onions, chopped

225g/8oz/1 cup ready-to-eat dried apricots, quartered

finely grated rind and juice of 1 orange

2.5ml/½ tsp turmeric

15ml/1 tbsp coriander seeds

15ml/1 tbsp salt

115g/4oz/1 cup flaked (sliced) almonds

1 Halve the butternut squash lengthways and scoop out the seeds. Peel off the skin, then cut the flesh into 2cm/¾in cubes.

2 Put the sugar and vinegar in a preserving pan and heat gently, stirring occasionally, until the sugar has dissolved.

3 Add the squash, onions, apricots, orange rind and juice, turmeric, coriander seeds and salt to the preserving pan. Bring the mixture slowly to the boil.

4 Reduce the heat and simmer gently for 45–50 minutes, stirring frequently towards the end of the cooking time, until the chutney is reduced to a thick consistency and no excess liquid remains. Stir in the flaked almonds.

5 Spoon the chutney into warmed sterilized jars, cover and seal. Store in a cool, dark place and allow to mature for at least 1 month before eating. Use within 2 years. Once opened, store in the refrigerator and use within 2 months.

VARIATION

If butternut squash is unavailable, use a wedge of pumpkin weighing about 500g/1¼lb instead.

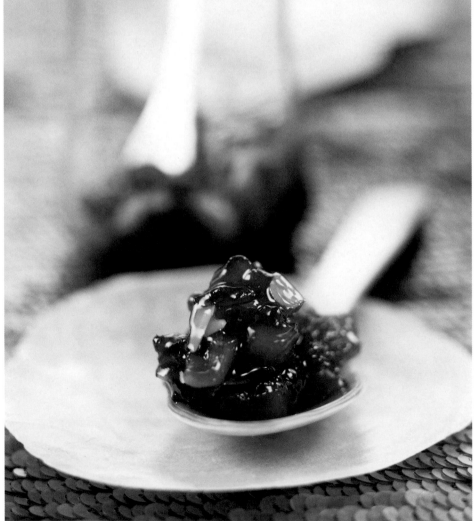

sweet and hot dried fruit chutney

This rich, thick and slightly sticky preserve of spiced dried fruit is a wonderful way to enliven cold roast turkey left over from Christmas or Thanksgiving dinners.

Makes about 1.5kg/3lb 6oz

INGREDIENTS

350g/12oz/1½ cups ready-to-eat dried apricots

225g/8oz/1⅓ cups dried dates, stoned (pitted)

225g/8oz/1⅓ cups dried figs

50g/2oz/⅓ cup glacé (candied) citrus peel

150g/5oz/1 cup raisins

50g/2oz/½ cup dried cranberries

120ml/4fl oz/½ cup cranberry juice

400ml/14fl oz/1⅔ cups cider vinegar

225g/8oz/1 cup demerara (raw) sugar

finely grated rind and juice of 1 lemon

5ml/1 tsp mixed spice (apple pie spice)

5ml/1 tsp ground coriander

5ml/1 tsp cayenne pepper

5ml/1 tsp salt

1 Roughly chop the dried apricots, dates, figs and citrus peel, then put all the dried fruit in a preserving pan. Pour over the cranberry juice, stir, then cover and leave to soak for 2 hours, or until the fruit has absorbed most of the juice.

2 Add the cider vinegar and sugar to the pan. Stir over a low heat until the sugar has dissolved.

3 Bring the mixture to the boil, then reduce the heat and simmer for about 30 minutes, or until the fruit is soft and the chutney fairly thick. Stir occasionally during cooking.

4 Stir in the lemon rind and juice, mixed spice, coriander, cayenne pepper and salt. Simmer for a further 15 minutes, stirring frequently towards the end of the cooking, until the chutney is thick and no excess liquid remains.

VARIATIONS

If you prefer, substitute dried sour cherries for the dried cranberries. Apple juice can be used instead of the cranberry juice.

5 Spoon the chutney into warmed sterilized jars, cover and seal. Store in a cool, dark place and allow to mature for at least 1 month before eating. Use within 1 year. Once opened, store in the refrigerator and use within 2 months.

pickled peach and chilli chutney

This is a spicy, rich chutney with a succulent texture. It is great served traditional-style, with cold roast meats such as ham, pork or turkey; it is also good with pan-fried chicken served in warm wraps. Try it with ricotta cheese as a filling for pitta bread.

Makes about 450g/1lb

INGREDIENTS

475ml/16fl oz/2 cups cider vinegar

275g/10oz/1¼ cups light muscovado (brown) sugar

225g/8oz/1⅓ cups dried dates, stoned (pitted) and finely chopped

5ml/1 tsp ground allspice

5ml/1 tsp ground mace

450g/1lb ripe peaches, stoned and cut into small chunks

3 onions, thinly sliced

4 fresh red chillies, seeded and finely chopped

4 garlic cloves, crushed

5cm/2in piece fresh root ginger, peeled and finely grated

5ml/1 tsp salt

1 Place the vinegar, sugar, dates, allspice and mace in a large pan and heat gently, stirring, until the sugar has dissolved. Bring to the boil, stirring occasionally.

2 Add the peaches, sliced onions, chopped chillies, crushed garlic, grated ginger and salt, and bring the mixture back to the boil, stirring occasionally.

3 Reduce the heat and simmer for 40–50 minutes, or until the chutney has thickened. Stir frequently to prevent the mixture sticking to the bottom of the pan.

4 Spoon the hot cooked chutney into warmed sterilized jars and seal immediately. When cold, store the jars in a cool, dark place and leave the chutney to mature for at least 2 weeks before eating. Use within 6 months.

COOK'S TIP

To test the consistency of the chutney before bottling, spoon a little of the mixture on to a plate; the chutney should hold its shape.

hot yellow plum chutney

It is well worth seeking out yellow plums to make this hot, fragrant chutney. They give it a slightly tart flavour and make it the perfect accompaniment to deep-fried Asian-style snacks such as spring rolls and wontons, or battered vegetables and shellfish.

Makes 1.3kg/3lb

INGREDIENTS

900g/2lb yellow plums, halved and stoned (pitted)

1 onion, finely chopped

7.5cm/3in piece fresh root ginger, peeled and grated

3 whole star anise

350ml/12fl oz/1½ cups white wine vinegar

225g/8oz/1 cup soft light brown sugar

5 celery sticks, thinly sliced

3 green chillies, seeded and finely sliced

2 garlic cloves, crushed

1 Put the halved plums, onion, ginger and star anise in a large pan and pour over half the white wine vinegar. Bring to the boil and simmer gently over a low heat for about 30 minutes, or until the plums have softened.

2 Stir the remaining vinegar, sugar, sliced celery, chillies and crushed garlic into the plum mixture. Cook very gently over a low heat, stirring frequently, until the sugar has completely dissolved.

3 Bring the mixture to the boil, then simmer for 45–50 minutes, or until thick, with no excess liquid. Stir frequently during the final stages of cooking to prevent the chutney sticking to the pan.

4 Spoon the plum chutney into warmed sterilized jars, then cover and seal immediately.

5 Store the chutney in a cool, dark place and allow to mature for at least 1 month before using. Use within 2 years.

COOK'S TIPS

• Once opened, store the chutney in the refrigerator and use within 3 months.

• Be sure to use jars with non-metallic lids to store the chutney.

mango chutney

No Indian meal would be complete without this classic chutney. Its gloriously sweet, tangy flavour complements the warm taste of Indian spices perfectly, but it is equally good scooped up on crispy fried popadoms. Mango chutney is also great served with chargrilled chicken, turkey or duck breasts; with potato wedges and soured cream; or spread on cheese on toast.

Makes about 1kg/2¼lb

INGREDIENTS

900g/2lb mangoes, halved, peeled and stoned

2.5ml/½ tsp salt

225g/8oz cooking apples, peeled

300ml/½ pint/1¼ cups distilled malt vinegar

200g/7oz/scant 1 cup demerara (raw) sugar

1 onion, chopped

1 garlic clove, crushed

10ml/2 tsp ground ginger

COOK'S TIPS

• Once opened, store the chutney in the refrigerator and use within 3 months.

• When serving mango chutney with crispy popadoms, also offer a selection of other condiments such as salty lime pickle, finely chopped fresh onion salad and minty yogurt.

1 Using a sharp knife, slice the mango flesh into chunks and place in a large, non-metallic bowl. Sprinkle with salt and set aside while you prepare the apples.

2 Using a sharp knife, cut the apples into quarters, then remove and discard the cores and peel. Chop the flesh roughly.

3 Put the malt vinegar and sugar in a preserving pan and heat very gently, stirring occasionally, until the sugar has dissolved completely.

4 Add the mangoes, apple, onion, garlic and ginger to the pan and slowly bring the mixture to the boil, stirring occasionally.

5 Reduce the heat and simmer gently for about 1 hour, stirring frequently towards the end of the cooking time, until the chutney is reduced to a thick consistency and no excess liquid remains.

6 Spoon the chutney into warmed sterilized jars, cover and seal. Store in a cool, dark place and allow to mature for at least 2 weeks before eating. Use within 1 year of making.

VARIATION

To make a chutney with a fiery, spicy kick to serve with cheeses and cold meats, seed and finely slice two green chillies and stir into the chutney with the garlic and ginger.

chunky pear and walnut chutney

This chutney recipe is ideal for using up hard windfall pears. Its mellow flavour is excellent with cheese and also good with grains such as in pilaff or with tabbouleh.

Makes about 1.8kg/4lb

INGREDIENTS

1.2kg/2½lb firm pears
225g/8oz tart cooking apples
225g/8oz onions
450ml/¾ pint/scant 2 cups cider vinegar
175g/6oz/generous 1 cup sultanas
 (golden raisins)
finely grated rind and juice
 of 1 orange
400g/14oz/2 cups granulated sugar
115g/4oz/1 cup walnuts,
 roughly chopped
2.5ml/½ tsp ground cinnamon

1 Peel and core the fruit, then chop into 2.5cm/1in chunks. Peel and quarter the onions, then chop into pieces the same size. Place in a preserving pan with the vinegar.

2 Slowly bring to the boil, then reduce the heat and simmer for 40 minutes, until the apples, pears and onions are tender, stirring the mixture occasionally.

3 Meanwhile, put the sultanas in a small bowl, pour over the orange juice and leave to soak.

4 Add the sugar, sultanas, and orange rind and juice to the pan. Gently heat until the sugar has dissolved, then simmer for 30–40 minutes, or until the chutney is thick and no excess liquid remains. Stir frequently towards the end of cooking to prevent the chutney sticking on the bottom of the pan.

5 Gently toast the walnuts in a non-stick pan over a low heat for 5 minutes, stirring frequently, until lightly coloured. Stir the nuts into the chutney with the cinnamon.

6 Spoon the chutney into warmed sterilized jars, cover and seal. Store in a cool, dark place and leave to mature for at least 1 month. Use within 1 year.

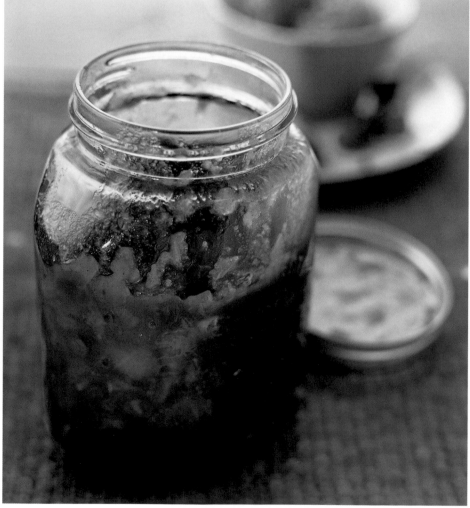

green grape chutney

A hint of lime heightens the fragrant grape flavour and complements the sweetness of this chutney. It is delicious warmed with a knob of butter and served with roast pork.

Makes 1.2kg/2½lb

INGREDIENTS

900g/2lb/6 cups seedless green grapes
900g/2lb tart cooking apples
450g/1lb/2¼ cups granulated sugar
450ml/¾ pint/scant 2 cups white
 wine vinegar
finely grated rind and juice
 of 1 lime
1.5ml/¼ tsp salt

COOK'S TIP

Once opened, store the chutney in the refrigerator and use within 1 month.

1 Halve the grapes if large, then peel, core and finely chop the apples. Put the fruit in a preserving pan with the sugar and vinegar and slowly bring to the boil.

2 Reduce the heat and simmer the chutney for about 45 minutes, or until the fruit is tender and the chutney fairly thick.

3 Stir the lime rind and juice and salt into the chutney and simmer for 15 minutes until the chutney is thick and no excess liquid remains.

4 Spoon the chutney into warmed sterilized jars, cover and seal. Store in a cool, dark place and leave to mature for at least 1 month before eating. Use within 18 months.

beetroot and orange preserve

With its vibrant red colour and rich earthy flavour, this distinctive chutney is good with salads as well as full-flavoured cheeses such as mature Cheddar, Stilton or Gorgonzola. You might also like to try it with cream cheese in baked potatoes.

Makes about 1.4kg/3lb

INGREDIENTS

350g/12oz raw beetroot (beets)

350g/12oz eating apples

300ml/½ pint/1¼ cups malt vinegar

200g/7oz/1 cup granulated sugar

225g/8oz red onions, finely chopped

1 garlic clove, crushed

finely grated rind and juice of 2 oranges

5ml/1 tsp ground allspice

5ml/1 tsp salt

1 Scrub or, if necessary, thinly peel the beetroot, then cut into 1cm/½in pieces. Peel, quarter and core the apples and cut into 1cm/½in pieces.

2 Put the vinegar and sugar in a preserving pan and heat gently, stirring occasionally, until the sugar has dissolved.

3 Add the beetroot, apples, onions, garlic, orange rind and juice, ground allspice and salt to the pan. Bring to the boil, reduce the heat, then simmer for 40 minutes.

4 Increase the heat slightly and boil for 10 minutes, or until the chutney is thick and no excess liquid remains. Stir frequently to prevent the chutney catching on the base of the pan.

5 Spoon the chutney into warmed sterilized jars, cover and seal. Store in a cool, dark place and allow to mature for at least 2 weeks before eating. Use within 6 months of making. Refrigerate once opened and use within 1 month.

COOK'S TIP

For speedy preparation and a fine-textured chutney, put the peeled beetroot through the coarse grating blade of a food processor.

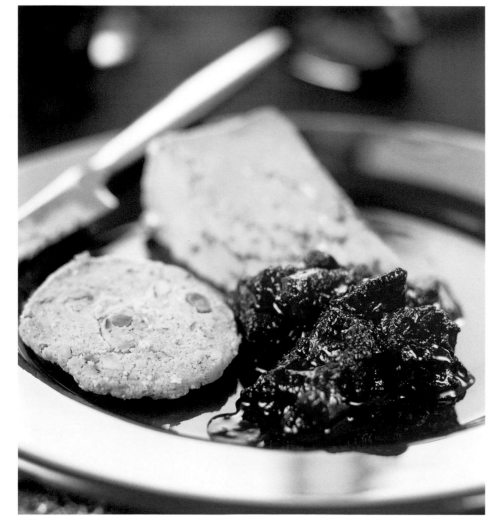

rhubarb and tangerine chutney

The rhubarb in this soft-textured chutney is added partway through the cooking, so that it retains its attractive colour and shape. It works especially well when partnered with Chinese-style roast duck, or with cold meats such as ham or gammon.

Makes about 1.3kg/3lb

INGREDIENTS

1 large onion, finely chopped

300ml/½ pint/1¼ cups distilled
  malt vinegar

4 whole cloves

7.5cm/3in cinnamon stick

1 tangerine

400g/14oz/2 cups granulated sugar

150g/5oz/1 cup sultanas (golden raisins)

1kg/2¼lb rhubarb, cut into
  2.5cm/1in lengths

1 Put the onion in a preserving pan with the vinegar, whole cloves and cinnamon stick. Bring to the boil, then reduce the heat and simmer for 10 minutes, or until the onions are just tender.

2 Meanwhile, thinly pare the rind from the tangerine. (It is often easier to peel the fruit first, then slice the white pith from the rind.) Finely shred the rind.

3 Add the tangerine rind, sugar and sultanas to the pan. Stir until all the sugar has dissolved, then simmer for 10 minutes, or until the syrup is thick.

4 Add the rhubarb to the pan. Cook gently for about 15 minutes, stirring carefully from time to time, until the rhubarb is soft but still retains its shape, and just a little spare liquid remains.

5 Remove the pan from the heat and leave to cool for 10 minutes, then stir gently to distribute the fruit. Spoon the chutney into warmed sterilized jars, cover and seal. Store in a cool, dark place and allow to mature for at least 1 month. Use within 1 year. Once opened, store in the refrigerator and use within 2 months.

COOK'S TIP

The finely shredded rind of half an orange may be used in place of the shredded tangerine rind.

relishes

These versatile condiments can be fresh and quick to prepare or rich and slowly simmered. They usually have bold, striking flavours with a piquant, sharp and spicy taste balanced by sweet and tangy tones. They are perfect for serving with cheese, cold or grilled meats or for jazzing up plain sandwich fillings.

tart tomato relish

Adding lime to this relish gives it a wonderfully tart, tangy flavour and a pleasantly sour after-taste. It is particularly good served with grilled or roast meats such as pork or lamb.

Makes about 500g/1¼lb

INGREDIENTS

2 pieces preserved stem ginger

1 lime

450g/1lb cherry tomatoes

115g/4oz/½ cup muscovado (molasses) sugar

120ml/4fl oz/½ cup white wine vinegar

5ml/1 tsp salt

VARIATION

Use chopped tomatoes in place of the cherry tomatoes, if you prefer.

1 Coarsely chop the preserved stem ginger. Slice the lime thinly, including the rind, then chop the slices into small pieces.

2 Place the cherry tomatoes, sugar, vinegar, salt, ginger and lime in a large heavy pan.

3 Bring the mixture to the boil, stirring until the sugar dissolves, then simmer rapidly for about 45 minutes. Stir frequently until the liquid has evaporated and the relish is thick and pulpy.

4 Leave the relish to cool for about 5 minutes, then spoon into sterilized jars. Leave to cool, then cover and store in the refrigerator for up to 1 month.

COOK'S TIP

There is always discussion between preserving enthusiasts as to the best choice of covering for chutneys and pickles. While cellophane covers are vinegarproof, they are difficult to secure for a good airtight seal, and not very good once opened. Screw-top lids with a plastic coating inside are best: put them on as soon as the piping hot preserve is potted and they will provide a hygienic, air-tight seal. New lids can be purchased for standard-size glass jars.

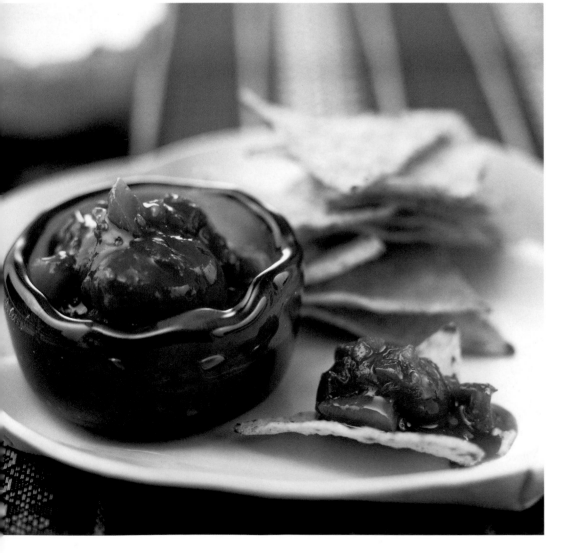

red hot relish

Make this relish during the summer months when tomatoes and peppers are plentiful. It enhances simple, plain dishes such as a cheese or mushroom omelette.

Makes about 1.3kg/3lb

800g/1¾lb ripe tomatoes, skinned
  and quartered

450g/1lb red onions, chopped

3 red (bell) peppers, seeded
  and chopped

3 fresh red chillies, seeded
  and finely sliced

200g/7oz/1 cup granulated sugar

200ml/7fl oz/scant 1 cup red
  wine vinegar

30ml/2 tbsp mustard seeds

10ml/2 tsp celery seeds

15ml/1 tbsp paprika

5ml/1 tsp salt

1 Put the chopped tomatoes, onions, peppers and chillies in a preserving pan, cover with a lid and cook over a very low heat for about 10 minutes, stirring once or twice, until the tomato juices start to run.

2 Add the sugar and vinegar to the tomato mixture and slowly bring to the boil, stirring occasionally until the sugar has dissolved completely. Add the mustard seeds, celery seeds, paprika and salt and stir well to combine.

3 Increase the heat under the pan slightly and cook the relish, uncovered, for about 30 minutes, or until most of the liquid has evaporated and the mixture has a thick, but moist consistency. Stir frequently towards the end of cooking time to prevent the mixture sticking to the pan.

4 Spoon the relish into warmed sterilized jars, cover and seal. Store in a cool, dark place and leave to mature for at least 2 weeks before eating. Use the relish within 1 year of making.

COOK'S TIP
Once opened, store the relish in the refrigerator and use within 2 months.

bloody mary relish

This fresh-tasting relish with contrasting textures of tomatoes, celery and cucumber is perfect for al fresco *summer eating. For a special occasion, serve it with freshly shucked oysters.*

Makes about 1.3kg/3lb

INGREDIENTS

1.3kg/3lb ripe well-flavoured tomatoes

1 large cucumber

30–45ml/2–3 tbsp salt

2 celery sticks, chopped

2 garlic cloves, peeled and crushed

175ml/6fl oz/¾ cup white wine vinegar

15ml/1 tbsp granulated sugar

60ml/4 tbsp vodka

5ml/1 tsp Tabasco sauce

10ml/2 tsp Worcestershire sauce

COOK'S TIP

To skin the tomatoes, plunge them in a bowl of just-boiled water for 30 seconds. The skins will split and will be easy to peel off.

1 Skin and chop the tomatoes. Peel the cucumber and slice the flesh from around the seeds. Discard the seeds and chop the flesh. Layer the vegetables in a colander placed over a bowl, lightly sprinkling each layer with salt. Cover, put in the refrigerator and leave to drain overnight.

2 The next day, rinse the tomatoes and cucumber thoroughly under cold running water to remove as much salt as possible. Drain well, then place in a pan. Discard the salty vegetable juices in the bowl.

3 Add the celery, garlic, vinegar and sugar to the pan and slowly bring to the boil over a low heat.

4 Cook the vegetables, uncovered, for about 30 minutes, stirring occasionally, until the vegetables have softened and most of the liquid has evaporated.

5 Remove the pan from the heat and leave to cool for about 5 minutes. Add the vodka, and Tabasco and Worcestershire sauces and stir well to combine.

6 Spoon the hot relish into warmed sterilized jars, cool, cover and seal. Store in the refrigerator for at least 1 week.

COOK'S TIP

Use the relish within 3 months. Once opened, store it in the refrigerator and use within 1 month.

yellow pepper and coriander relish

Fresh relishes are quick and easy to make although they do not have a long shelf life. Try this relish with mild, creamy cheeses or with grilled tuna or other firm fish, poultry or meat.

Makes 1 small jar

INGREDIENTS

1 large yellow (bell) pepper

45ml/3 tbsp sesame oil

1 large mild fresh red chilli

small handful of fresh coriander (cilantro)

salt

1 Seed and coarsely chop the yellow peppers. Heat the oil in a pan, add the peppers and cook, stirring frequently, for 8–10 minutes, until lightly coloured.

2 Meanwhile, seed the chilli, slice it very thinly and set aside. Transfer the peppers to a food processor and process until chopped, but not puréed. Transfer half the peppers to a bowl, leaving the rest in the food processor.

3 Using a sharp knife, chop the fresh coriander, then add it to the mixture in the food processor and process briefly to combine. Tip the mixture into the bowl with the rest of the peppers, add the sliced chilli and stir well to combine.

4 Season the relish with salt to taste and stir well to combine. Cover the bowl with clear film (plastic wrap) and chill in the refrigerator until ready to serve.

COOK'S TIPS

• Red and orange sweet peppers work just as well as yellow, though green peppers are unsuitable as they are not sweet enough in flavour.

• This relish does not keep well, so use within 3 or 4 days of making.

• If you find the flavour of chilli too hot, use only half a chilli and chop into tiny pieces.

sweet piccalilli

Undoubtedly one of the most popular relishes, piccalilli can be eaten with grilled sausages, ham or chops, cold meats or a strong, well-flavoured cheese such as Cheddar. It should contain a good selection of fresh crunchy vegetables in a smooth, mustard sauce.

Makes about 1.8kg/4lb

INGREDIENTS

1 large cauliflower

450g/1lb pickling (pearl) onions

900g/2lb mixed vegetables, such as marrow (large zucchini), cucumber, French (green) beans

225g/8oz/1 cup salt

2.4 litres/4 pints/10 cups cold water

200g/7oz/1 cup granulated sugar

2 garlic cloves, peeled and crushed

10ml/2 tsp mustard powder

5ml/1 tsp ground ginger

1 litre/1¾ pints/4 cups distilled (white) vinegar

25g/1oz/¼ cup plain (all-purpose) flour

15ml/1 tbsp turmeric

1 Prepare the vegetables. Divide the cauliflower into small florets; peel and quarter the pickling onions; seed and finely dice the marrow and cucumber; top and tail the French beans, then cut them into 2.5cm/1in lengths.

2 Layer the vegetables in a large glass or stainless steel bowl, generously sprinkling each layer with salt. Pour over the water, cover the bowl with clear film (plastic wrap) and leave to soak for about 24 hours.

3 Drain the soaked vegetables, and discard the brine. Rinse well in several changes of cold water to remove as much salt as possible, then drain them thoroughly.

4 Put the sugar, garlic, mustard, ginger and 900ml/1½ pints/3¾ cups of the vinegar in a preserving pan. Heat gently, stirring occasionally, until the sugar has dissolved.

5 Add the vegetables to the pan, bring to the boil, reduce the heat and simmer for 10–15 minutes, or until they are almost tender.

6 Mix the flour and turmeric with the remaining vinegar and stir into the vegetables. Bring to the boil, stirring, and simmer for 5 minutes, until the piccalilli is thick.

7 Spoon the piccalilli into warmed sterilized jars, cover and seal. Store in a cool, dark place for at least 2 weeks. Use within 1 year.

corn relish

*When golden corn cobs are in season, try preserving their kernels in this delicious relish.
It has a lovely crunchy texture and a wonderfully bright, appetizing appearance.*

Makes about 1kg/2¼lb

INGREDIENTS

6 large fresh corn on the cob

½ small white cabbage, weighing about 275g/10oz, very finely shredded

2 small onions, halved and very finely sliced

475ml/16fl oz/2 cups distilled malt vinegar

200g/7oz/1 cup golden granulated sugar

1 red (bell) pepper, seeded and finely chopped

5ml/1 tsp salt

15ml/1 tbsp plain (all-purpose) flour

5ml/1 tsp mustard powder

2.5ml/½ tsp turmeric

1 Put the corn in a pan of boiling water and cook for 2 minutes. Drain and, when cool enough to handle, use a sharp knife to strip the kernels from the cobs.

2 Put the corn kernels in a pan with the cabbage and onions. Reserve 30ml/2 tbsp of the vinegar, then add the rest to the pan with the sugar. Slowly bring to the boil, stirring occasionally until the sugar dissolves. Simmer for 15 minutes. Add the red pepper and simmer for a further 10 minutes.

3 Blend the salt, flour, mustard and turmeric with the reserved vinegar to make a smooth paste.

4 Stir the paste into the vegetable mixture and bring back to the boil. Simmer for 5 minutes, until the mixture has thickened.

5 Spoon the relish into warmed sterilized jars, cover and seal. Store in a cool dark place. Use within 6 months of making. Once opened, store in the refrigerator and use within 2 months.

COOK'S TIP

This tangy relish is the perfect barbecue preserve. It is perfect for enlivening barbecued meats such as chicken, sausages and burgers.

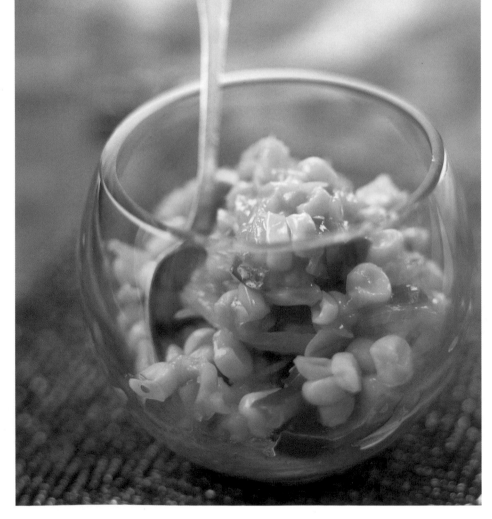

cool cucumber and green tomato relish

This is a great way to use up those green tomatoes that seem as though they're never going to ripen. Combined with cucumber, they make a pale green relish that is great for barbecues.

Makes about 1.6kg/3½lb

INGREDIENTS

2 cucumbers

900g/2lb green tomatoes

4 onions

7.5ml/1½ tsp salt

350ml/12fl oz/1½ cups distilled (white) vinegar

150g/5oz/scant ¾ cup demerara (raw) sugar

200g/7oz/1 cup granulated sugar

15ml/1 tbsp plain (all-purpose) flour

2.5ml/½ tsp mustard powder

1 Wash the cucumbers and green tomatoes. Cut into 1cm/½in cubes. Peel and finely chop the onions.

2 Layer the vegetables in a strainer or colander placed over a bowl, lightly sprinkling each layer with salt, then cover and leave to drain for at least 6 hours, or overnight.

3 Discard the salty liquid and tip the salted vegetables into a large heavy pan. Reserve 30ml/2 tbsp of the vinegar and add the rest to the pan with the demerara and granulated sugars.

4 Slowly bring the vegetable mixture to the boil, stirring occasionally until the sugar has dissolved completely. Reduce the heat slightly and cook, uncovered, for about 30 minutes, or until the vegetables are tender.

5 In a small bowl, blend the flour and mustard to a paste with the reserved vinegar. Stir the mixture into the relish and simmer for about 20 minutes, or until the mixture is very thick.

6 Spoon the relish into warmed sterilized jars, cover and seal. Store in a cool, dark place for at least 1 week. Use the relish within 6 months. Once opened, keep in the refrigerator and use within 2 months.

malay mixed vegetable relish

This traditional, full-flavoured relish, with its crunchy texture and spicy kick, is known as acar kuning *in Malaysia. It is served in very generous portions, almost like a side salad.*

Makes about 900g/2lb

INGREDIENTS

12 small pickling (pearl) onions, quartered

225g/8oz French (green) beans, cut into 2.5cm/1in lengths

225g/8oz carrots, cut into 2.5cm/1in long thin sticks

225g/8oz cauliflower, cut into small florets

5ml/1 tsp mustard powder

5ml/1 tsp salt

10ml/2 tsp granulated sugar

60ml/4 tbsp sesame seeds

For the spice paste

2 shallots, finely chopped

2 garlic cloves, crushed

2 fresh green chillies, seeded and finely chopped

115g/4oz/1 cup dry-roasted peanuts

5ml/1 tsp turmeric

5ml/1 tsp chilli powder

60ml/4 tbsp distilled (white) vinegar

30ml/2 tbsp vegetable oil

175ml/6fl oz/¾ cup boiling water

1 Make the spice paste. Put the shallots, garlic, chillies, peanuts, turmeric, chilli powder, vinegar and oil in a food processor or blender and process to a fairly smooth paste.

2 Transfer the mixture to a large heavy pan and slowly bring to the boil. Reduce the heat and simmer gently for 2 minutes, stirring all the time. Gradually stir in the water and simmer the mixture for a further 3 minutes.

3 Add the onions to the pan, cover and simmer for 5 minutes, then add the beans and carrots. Cover the pan again and cook for a further 3 minutes.

4 Finally, add the cauliflower, mustard, salt and sugar to the pan and simmer, uncovered, for about 5 minutes, or until the vegetables are tender and have absorbed most of the sauce. Remove the pan from the heat and set aside to cool for a few minutes.

5 Meanwhile, toast the sesame seeds in a non-stick pan over a medium heat until golden, stirring frequently. Stir the seeds into the vegetable mixture.

6 Spoon the relish into warmed sterilized jars, cover and seal. Leave until completely cold, then store in the refrigerator.

COOK'S TIP

The relish can be served immediately and should be used within 4 weeks.

carrot and almond relish

This is a Middle Eastern classic, usually made with long fine strands of carrot, available from many supermarkets. Alternatively, grate large carrots lengthways on a medium grater.

2 Put the lemon juice, vinegar, water, honey and salt in a jug (pitcher) and stir until the salt has dissolved. Pour over the carrot mixture. Mix well, cover and leave in the refrigerator for 4 hours.

3 Transfer the chilled mixture to a preserving pan. Slowly bring to the boil, then reduce the heat and simmer for 15 minutes until the carrots and ginger are tender.

4 Increase the heat and boil for 15 minutes, or until most of the liquid has evaporated and the mixture is thick. Stir frequently towards the end of the cooking time to prevent the mixture from sticking to the pan.

5 Put the almonds in a frying pan and toast over a low heat until just beginning to colour. Gently stir into the relish, taking care not to break the almonds.

Makes about 675g/1½lb

INGREDIENTS

15ml/1 tbsp coriander seeds

500g/1¼lb carrots, grated

50g/2oz fresh root ginger, finely shredded

200g/7oz/1 cup caster (superfine) sugar

finely grated rind and juice of 1 lemon

120ml/4fl oz/½ cup white wine vinegar

75ml/5 tbsp water

30ml/2 tbsp clear honey

7.5ml/1½ tsp salt

50g/2oz/½ cup flaked (sliced) almonds

1 Crush the coriander seeds using a mortar and pestle. Put them in a bowl with the carrots, ginger, sugar and lemon rind and mix together well to combine.

6 Spoon the relish into warmed sterilized jars, cover and seal. Leave for at least 1 month and use within 18 months. Once opened, store in the refrigerator.

lemon and garlic relish

This powerful relish is flavoured with North African spices and punchy preserved lemons, which are widely available in Middle Eastern stores. It is great served with Moroccan tagines.

Makes 1 small jar

INGREDIENTS

45ml/3 tbsp olive oil

3 large red onions, sliced

2 heads of garlic, separated into cloves and peeled

10ml/2 tsp coriander seeds, crushed

10ml/2 tsp light muscovado (brown) sugar, plus a little extra

pinch of saffron threads

5cm/2in piece cinnamon stick

2–3 small whole dried red chillies (optional)

2 fresh bay leaves

30–45ml/2–3 tbsp sherry vinegar

juice of ½ small orange

30ml/2 tbsp chopped preserved lemon

salt and ground black pepper

1 Gently heat the oil in a large heavy pan. Add the onions and stir, then cover and cook on the lowest setting for 10–15 minutes, stirring occasionally, until soft.

2 Add the garlic cloves and the coriander seeds. Cover and cook for 5–8 minutes, until soft.

3 Add a pinch of salt, lots of ground black pepper and the sugar to the onions and cook, uncovered, for a further 5 minutes.

4 Soak the saffron threads in about 45ml/3 tbsp warm water for 5 minutes, then add to the onions, with the soaking water. Add the cinnamon stick, dried chillies, if using, and bay leaves. Stir in 30ml/2 tbsp of the sherry vinegar and the orange juice.

5 Cook very gently, uncovered, until the onions are very soft and most of the liquid evaporated. Stir in the preserved lemon and cook gently for 5 minutes.

6 Taste the relish and adjust the seasoning, adding more salt, sugar and/or vinegar to taste.

7 Serve warm or cold (not hot or chilled). The relish tastes best if left to stand for 24 hours.

COOK'S TIP

You can store the relish in a tightly covered bowl or jar for up to a week in the refrigerator. Allow it to stand at room temperature for about an hour before serving.

cranberry and red onion relish

This wine-enriched relish is perfect for serving with hot roast turkey at Christmas or Thanksgiving. It is also good served with cold meats or stirred into a beef or game casserole for a touch of sweetness. It can be made several months in advance of the festive season.

Makes about 900g/2lb

INGREDIENTS

450g/1lb small red onions

30ml/2 tbsp olive oil

225g/8oz/1 cup soft light
  brown sugar

450g/1lb/4 cups fresh or
  frozen cranberries

120ml/4fl oz/½ cup red wine vinegar

120ml/4fl oz/½ cup red wine

15ml/1 tbsp mustard seeds

2.5ml/½ tsp ground ginger

30ml/2 tbsp orange liqueur or port

salt and ground black pepper

VARIATION

Redcurrants make a very good substitute for cranberries in this recipe. They produce a relish with a lovely flavour and pretty colour.

1 Halve the red onions and slice them very thinly. Heat the oil in a large pan, add the onions and cook them over a very low heat for about 15 minutes, stirring occasionally until softened. Add 30ml/2 tbsp of the sugar and cook for a further 5 minutes, or until the onions are caramelized.

4 Increase the heat slightly and cook uncovered for a further 10 minutes, stirring the mixture frequently until it is well reduced and thickened. Remove the pan from the heat, then season with salt and pepper to taste.

2 Meanwhile, put the cranberries in a pan with the remaining sugar, and the vinegar, red wine, mustard seeds and ginger. Heat gently until the sugar has dissolved, then cover and bring to the boil.

3 Simmer the relish mixture for 12–15 minutes, until the berries have burst and are tender, then stir in the caramelized onions.

5 Transfer the relish to warmed sterilized jars. Spoon a little of the orange liqueur or port over the top of each, then cover and seal. Store in a cool place for up to 6 months. Store in the refrigerator once opened and use within 1 month.

COOK'S TIP

It is important to cover the pan when cooking the cranberries because they can sometimes pop out of the pan during cooking and are very hot.

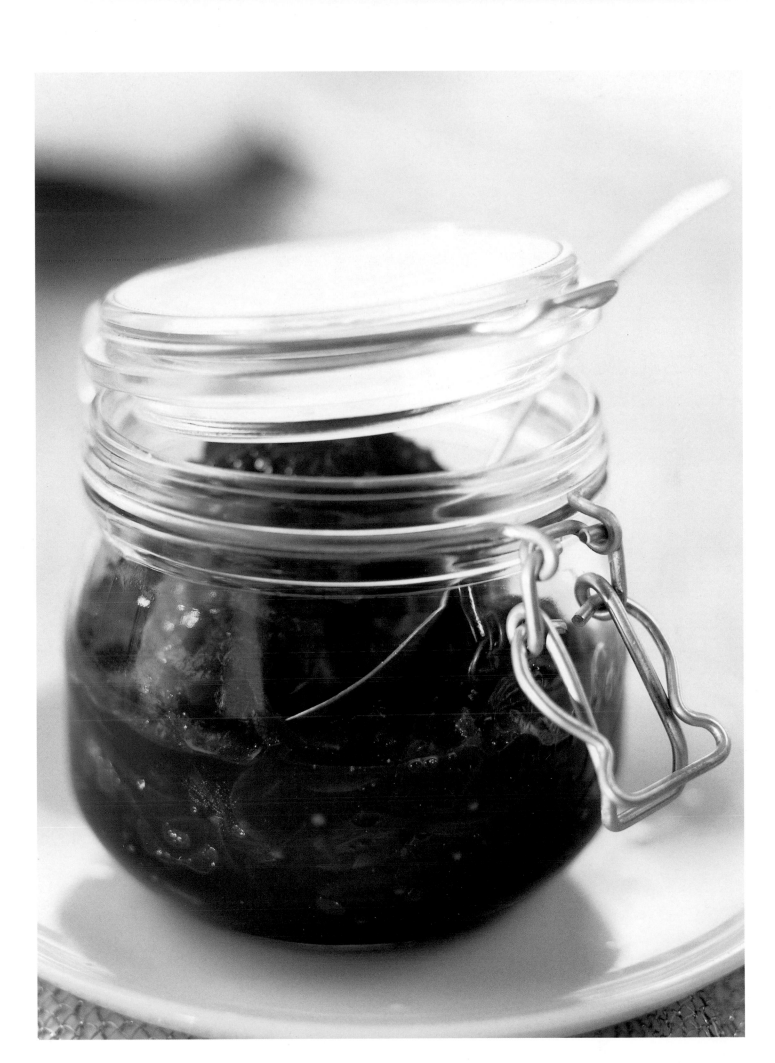

mango and papaya relish

Brightly coloured pieces of dried papaya adds taste and texture to this anise-spiced mango preserve. The fruit is cooked for only a short time to retain its juicy texture and fresh flavour.

Makes about 800g/1¾lb

INGREDIENTS

115g/4oz/½ cup dried papaya

30ml/2 tbsp orange or
 apple juice

2 large slightly underripe mangoes

2 shallots, very finely sliced

4cm/1½in piece fresh root
 ginger, grated

1 garlic clove, crushed

2 whole star anise

150ml/¼ pint/⅔ cup cider vinegar

75g/3oz/scant ½ cup light muscovado
 (brown) sugar

1.5ml/¼ tsp salt

1 Using a sharp knife or scissors, roughly chop the papaya and place in a small bowl. Sprinkle over the orange or apple juice and leave to soak for at least 10 minutes.

2 Meanwhile, peel and slice the mangoes, cutting the flesh away from the stone (pit) in large slices. Cut into 1cm/½in chunks, then set the flesh aside.

3 Put the sliced shallots, ginger, garlic and star anise in a large pan. Pour over the vinegar. Slowly bring to the boil, then reduce the heat, cover and simmer for 5 minutes, or until the shallots are just beginning to soften.

4 Add the sugar and salt to the pan and stir over a low heat until dissolved. When the mixture is simmering, add the papaya and mango and cook for a further 20 minutes, or until the fruit is just tender and the relish mixture has reduced and thickened.

5 Allow the relish to cool for about 5 minutes, then spoon into warmed sterilized jars. Allow to cool completely before covering and sealing. Store in a cool, dark place and use within 3 months of making. Once opened, keep the jars in the refrigerator and use within 1 month.

sweet and sour pineapple relish

This simple preserve is an excellent condiment for perking up grilled chicken or bacon chops. Using canned pineapple means it can be made mainly from store-cupboard ingredients.

Makes about 675g/1½lb

INGREDIENTS

2 x 400g/14oz cans pineapple rings
  or pieces in natural juice

1 lemon

115g/4oz/½ cup granulated sugar

45m/3 tbsp white wine vinegar

6 spring onions (scallions),
  finely chopped

2 fresh red chillies, seeded and
  finely chopped

salt and ground black pepper

1 Drain the pineapple, reserving 120ml/4fl oz/½ cup of the juice. Pour the juice into a preserving pan. Finely chop the pineapple, if necessary, and place in a sieve (strainer) set over a bowl.

2 Pare a strip of rind from the lemon. Squeeze the lemon juice and add to the pan with the lemon rind, sugar and vinegar.

3 Heat over a low heat, stirring occasionally, until the sugar has dissolved, then bring to the boil. Cook, uncovered, over a medium heat for about 10 minutes, or until the sauce has thickened slightly.

4 Add the chopped onions and chillies to the pan, together with any juice that has been drained from the chopped pineapple.

5 Cook the sauce for 5 minutes, until thick and syrupy, stirring frequently towards the end of the cooking time.

6 Increase the heat slightly, add the pineapple and cook for about 4 minutes, or until most of the liquid has evaporated. Season.

7 Spoon the relish into warmed sterilized jars, cover and seal. Store in the refrigerator and eat within 3 months of making.

plum and cherry relish

This simple sweet and sour fruity relish complements rich poultry, game or meat such as roast duck or grilled duck breasts. Sieve a few spoonfuls into a sauce or gravy to add fruity zest and flavour, as well as additional colour.

Makes about 350g/12oz

INGREDIENTS

350g/12oz dark-skinned red plums

350g/12oz/2 cups cherries

2 shallots, finely chopped

15ml/1 tbsp olive oil

30ml/2 tbsp dry sherry

60ml/4 tbsp red wine vinegar

15ml/1 tbsp balsamic vinegar

1 bay leaf

90g/3½oz/scant ½ cup demerara (raw) sugar

1 Halve and stone (pit) the plums, then roughly chop the flesh. Stone all the cherries.

2 Cook the shallots gently in the oil for 5 minutes, or until soft. Add the fruit, sherry, vinegars, bay leaf and sugar.

3 Slowly bring the mixture to the boil, stirring until the sugar has dissolved completely. Increase the heat and cook briskly for about 15 minutes, or until the relish is very thick and the fruit tender.

4 Remove the bay leaf and spoon the relish into warmed sterilized jars. Cover and seal. Store the relish in the refrigerator and use within 3 months.

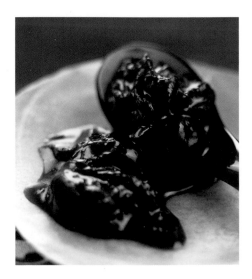

nectarine relish

This sweet and tangy fruit relish goes very well with hot roast meats such as pork and game birds such as guinea fowl and pheasant. Make it while nectarines are plentiful and keep tightly covered in the refrigerator to serve for Christmas, or even to give as a seasonal gift.

Makes about 450g/1lb

INGREDIENTS

45ml/3 tbsp olive oil

2 Spanish (Bermuda) onions, thinly sliced

1 fresh green chilli, seeded and
  finely chopped

5ml/1 tsp finely chopped fresh rosemary

2 bay leaves

450g/1lb nectarines, stoned (pitted) and
  cut into chunks

150g/5oz/1 cup raisins

10ml/2 tsp crushed coriander seeds

350g/12oz/1½ cups demerara
  (raw) sugar

200ml/7fl oz/scant 1 cup red
  wine vinegar

1 Heat the oil in a large pan. Add the onions, chilli, rosemary and bay leaves. Cook, stirring frequently, for about 15 minutes, or until the onions are soft.

COOK'S TIP

Pots of this relish make a lovely gift. Store it in pretty jars and add a colourful label identifying the relish, and reminding the recipient that it should be stored in the refrigerator, and when it should be used by.

2 Add the nectarines, raisins, coriander seeds, sugar and vinegar to the pan, then slowly bring to the boil, stirring frequently.

3 Reduce the heat under the pan and simmer gently for 1 hour, or until the relish is thick and sticky. Stir occasionally during cooking, and more frequently towards the end of cooking time to prevent the relish sticking to the pan.

4 Spoon the relish into warmed, sterilized jars and seal. Leave the jars to cool completely, then store in the refrigerator. The relish will keep well in the refrigerator for up to 5 months.

savoury jellies

Although many of the jellies in this chapter contain sugar, they are all prepared as a condiment to serve with savoury foods such as meat, fish or cheese. Soft or firmly set, these interesting jellies are made from fruits and vegetables and usually have a tangy, sweet-and-sour taste. Many are flavoured with zesty citrus fruits and are spiked with herbs and spices to produce wonderful aromatic flavours. They really are a true gourmet treat – enjoy!

lemon grass and ginger jelly

This aromatic jelly is delicious with Asian-style roast meat and poultry such as Chinese crispy duck. It is also the perfect foil for rich fish, especially cold smoked trout or mackerel.

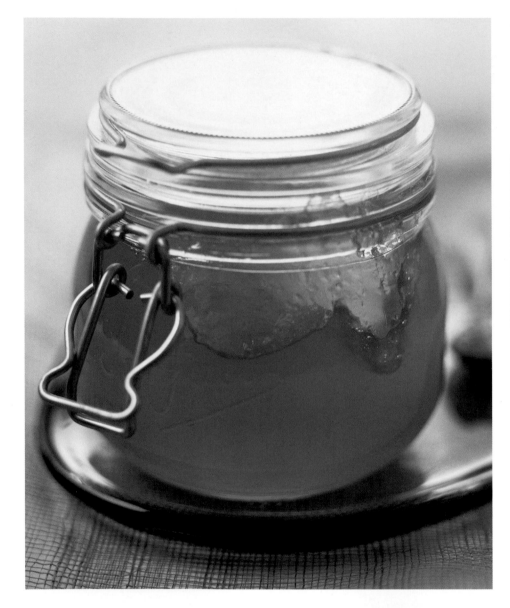

2 Put the chopped lemon grass in a preserving pan and pour over the water. Add the lemons and ginger. Bring to the boil, then reduce the heat, cover and simmer for 1 hour, or until the lemons are pulpy.

3 Pour the fruit and juices into a sterilized jelly bag suspended over a large bowl. Leave to drain for at least 3 hours, or until the juice stops dripping.

4 Measure the juice into the cleaned preserving pan, adding 450g/1lb/2¼ cups sugar for every 600ml/1 pint/2½ cups juice.

5 Heat the mixture gently, stirring occasionally, until the sugar has dissolved completely. Boil rapidly for about 10 minutes until the jelly reaches setting point (105°C/220°F). Remove from the heat.

6 Skim any scum off the surface using a slotted spoon, then pour the jelly into warmed sterilized jars, cover and seal. Store in a cool, dark place and use within 1 year. Once opened, keep in the refrigerator. Eat within 3 months.

Makes about 900g/2lb

INGREDIENTS

2 lemon grass stalks

1.5 litres/2½ pints/6¼ cups water

1.3kg/3lb lemons, washed and cut into small pieces

50g/2oz fresh root ginger, unpeeled, thinly sliced

about 450g/1lb/2¼ cups preserving or granulated sugar

1 Using a rolling pin, bruise the lemon grass, then chop roughly.

roasted red pepper and chilli jelly

The hint of chilli in this glowing red jelly makes it ideal for spicing up hot or cold roast meat, sausages or hamburgers. The jelly is also good stirred into sauces or used as a glaze for poultry.

Makes about 900g/2lb

INGREDIENTS

8 red (bell) peppers, quartered
  and seeded
4 fresh red chillies, halved and seeded
1 onion, roughly chopped
2 garlic cloves, roughly chopped
250ml/8fl oz/1 cup water
250ml/8fl oz/1 cup white wine vinegar
7.5ml/1½ tsp salt
450g/1lb/2¼ cups preserving
  or granulated sugar
25ml/1½ tbsp powdered pectin

1 Arrange the peppers, skin side up, on a rack in a grill (broiling) pan and grill (broil) until the skins blister and blacken.

2 Put the peppers in a polythene bag until they are cool enough to handle, then remove the skins.

3 Put the skinned peppers, chillies, onion, garlic and water in a food processor or blender and process to a purée. Press the purée through a nylon sieve set over a bowl, pressing hard with a wooden spoon, to extract as much juice as possible. There should be about 750ml/1¼ pints/3 cups.

4 Scrape the purée into a large stainless steel pan, then stir in the white wine vinegar and salt.

5 In a bowl, combine the sugar and pectin, then stir it into the pepper mixture. Heat gently, stirring, until the sugar and pectin have dissolved completely, then bring to a rolling boil. Cook the jelly, stirring frequently, for exactly 4 minutes, then remove the pan from the heat.

6 Pour the jelly into warmed, sterilized jars. Leave to cool and set, then cover, label and store.

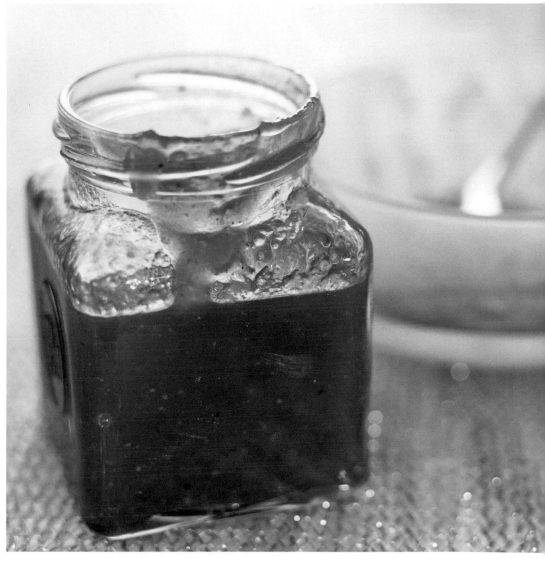

tomato and herb jelly

This dark golden jelly is delicious served with roast and grilled meats, especially lamb. It is also great for enlivening tomato-based pasta sauces: stirring a couple of teaspoons of the jelly into sauces helps to heighten their flavour and counteract acidity.

Makes about 1.3kg/3lb

INGREDIENTS

1.8kg/4lb tomatoes

2 lemons

2 bay leaves

300ml/½ pint/1¼ cups cold water

250ml/8fl oz/1 cup malt vinegar

bunch of fresh herbs such as rosemary, thyme, parsley and mint, plus a few extra sprigs for the jars

about 900g/2lb/4½ cups preserving or granulated sugar

COOK'S TIP

Once you have opened a jar of this jelly, store it in the refrigerator and use within 3 months.

1 Wash the tomatoes and lemons well, then cut the tomatoes into quarters and the lemons into small pieces. Put the chopped tomatoes and lemons in a large heavy pan with the bay leaves and pour over the water and vinegar.

4 Pour the tomato mixture and all the juices into a sterilized jelly bag suspended over a large bowl. Leave to drain for about 3 hours, or until the juices stop dripping.

5 Measure the juice into the cleaned pan, adding 450g/1lb/ 2¼ cups sugar for every 600ml/ 1 pint/2½ cups juice. Heat gently, stirring, until the sugar dissolves. Boil rapidly for 10 minutes, to setting point (105°C/220°F), then remove from the heat. Skim off any scum.

2 Add the herbs, either one herb or a mixture if preferred. (If you are using pungent woody herbs such as rosemary and thyme, use about six sprigs; if you are using milder leafy herbs such as parsley or mint, add about 12 large sprigs.)

3 Bring the mixture to the boil, then reduce the heat. Cover the pan with a lid and simmer for about 40 minutes, or until the tomatoes are very soft.

6 Leave the jelly for a few minutes until a skin forms. Place a herb sprig in each warmed sterilized jar, then pour in the jelly. Cover and seal when cold. Store in a cool, dark place and use within 1 year.

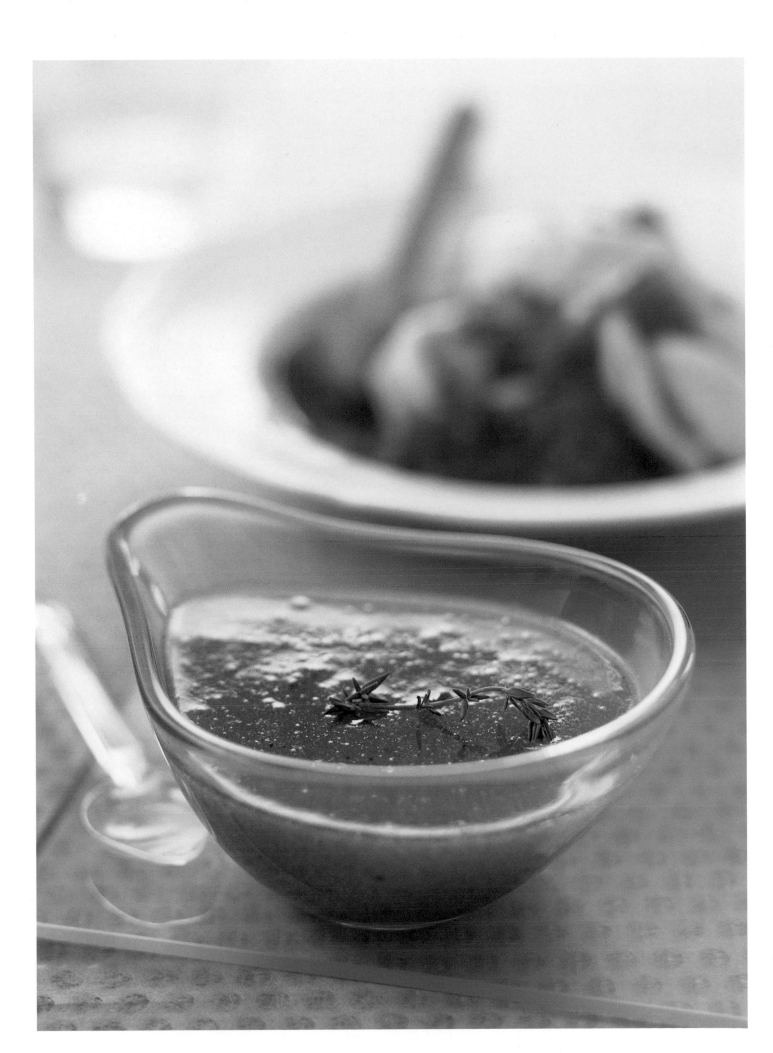

citrus thyme jelly

You can vary the sharpness of this jelly by altering the proportions of fruit. Use more oranges and fewer lemons and limes to obtain a milder, sweeter-tasting jelly.

2 Bring the mixture to the boil, then reduce the heat, cover and simmer for 1 hour, or until pulpy. Discard the bay leaves, then pour the fruit and juices into a sterilized jelly bag suspended over a large bowl. Leave to drain for 3 hours, or until the juices stop dripping.

3 Measure the juice into the cleaned pan, adding 450g/1lb/ 2¼ cups sugar for every 600ml/ 1 pint/2½ cups juice. Heat gently until the sugar has dissolved. Bring to the boil, then boil rapidly for about 10 minutes, or until setting point is reached (105°C/220°F). Remove the pan from the heat.

Makes about 1.3kg/3lb

INGREDIENTS

675g/1½lb lemons

675g/1½lb limes

450g/1lb oranges

2 bay leaves

2 litres/3½ pints/8¾ cups water

about 800g/1¾lb/4 cups preserving
 or granulated sugar

60ml/4 tbsp fresh thyme leaves

COOK'S TIP

It is important to stir the jelly before potting to re-distribute the herbs.

1 Wash all the fruit, then cut into small pieces. Place in a large heavy pan with the bay leaves and pour over the water.

4 Skim any scum off the surface, then stir in the thyme leaves. Leave to cool for a few minutes until a thin skin forms, then gently stir again to make sure the thyme is evenly distributed.

5 Pour the jelly into warmed sterilized jars. Cover and seal when cold. Store in a cool, dark place and use within 1 year. Once opened, store in the refrigerator and eat within 3 months.

bitter lime and juniper jelly

In this sharp, aromatic jelly the distinctive taste of zesty lime and the rich, resinous flavour of juniper berries is enhanced with a hint of aniseed from the splash of Pernod.

Makes about 1.6kg/3½lb

INGREDIENTS

6 limes

1.3kg/3lb tart cooking apples

6 juniper berries, crushed

1.75 litres/3 pints/7½ cups water

about 800g/1¾lb/4 cups preserving
  or granulated sugar

45ml/3 tbsp Pernod (optional)

1 Wash the limes and apples, then cut them into small pieces. Put them in a large heavy pan with the juniper berries. Pour over the water, then bring to the boil and simmer for about 1 hour, or until the fruit is very tender and pulpy.

2 Pour the fruit and juices into a sterilized jelly bag suspended over a large bowl. Leave the fruit to drain for at least 3 hours, until the juices stop dripping.

3 Measure the juice into the cleaned pan, adding 450g/1lb/ 2¼ cups sugar for every 600ml/ 1 pint/2½ cups juice. Heat gently, stirring occasionally, until the sugar has dissolved. Boil rapidly for about 10 minutes, to setting point (105°C/220°F), then remove the pan from the heat.

4 Skim any scum off the surface using a slotted spoon, then stir in the Pernod, if using. Pour the jelly into warmed sterilized jars, cover and seal immediately.

5 Store the jelly in a cool, dark place and use within 1 year. Once opened, keep in the refrigerator and eat within 3 months.

COOK'S TIP

When using citrus fruits for preserves, try to use unwaxed ones. If they are unavailable, scrub waxed fruits well.

apple, orange and cider jelly

A spoonful or two of this tangy amber jelly adds a real sparkle to a plate of cold meats, especially ham and pork or rich game pâtés. Tart cooking apples make the best-flavoured jelly, while the addition of cloves gives it a wonderfully warm, spicy taste and aroma.

Makes about 1.8kg/4lb

INGREDIENTS

1.3kg/3lb tart cooking apples

4 oranges

4 whole cloves

1.2 litres/2 pints/5 cups sweet cider

about 600ml/1 pint/2½ cups cold water

about 800g/1¾lb/4 cups preserving
 or granulated sugar

VARIATION

Replace some of the apples with crab apples for a more distinctive taste.

1 Wash and chop the apples and oranges, then put in a preserving pan with the cloves, cider and water to barely cover the fruit.

2 Bring the mixture to the boil, cover and simmer gently for 1 hour, stirring occasionally.

3 Pour the fruit and juices into a sterilized jelly bag suspended over a large bowl. Leave to drain for at least 4 hours, or overnight, until the juices stop dripping.

4 Measure the juice into the cleaned preserving pan, adding 450g/1lb/2¼ cups sugar for every 600ml/1 pint/2½ cups juice.

5 Heat the mixture gently stirring, until the sugar has dissolved. Boil rapidly for about 10 minutes until setting point is reached (105°C/220°F). Remove from the heat.

6 Skim any scum off the surface, then pour the jelly into warmed sterilized jars. Cover and seal. Store in a cool, dark place and use within 18 months. Once opened, store in the refrigerator and eat within 3 months.

quince and rosemary jelly

The amount of water needed for this jelly varies according to the ripeness of the fruit. For a good set, hard under-ripe quinces should be used as they contain the most pectin. If the fruit is soft and ripe, add a little lemon juice along with the water.

Makes about 900g/2lb

INGREDIENTS

900g/2lb quinces, cut into small pieces, with bruised parts removed

900ml–1.2 litres/1½–2 pints/ 3¾–5 cups water

lemon juice (optional)

4 large sprigs of fresh rosemary

about 900g/2lb/4½ cups preserving or granulated sugar

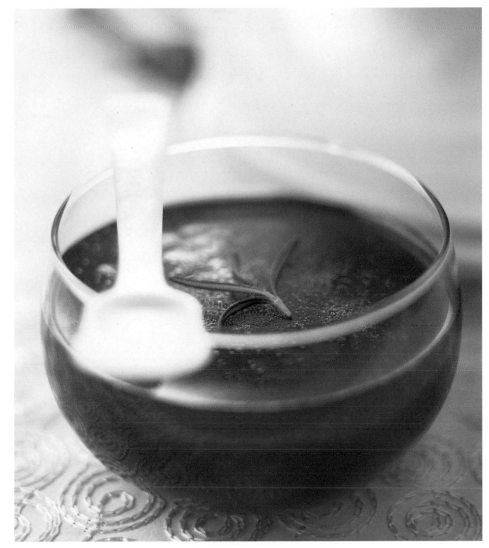

1 Put the chopped quinces in a large heavy pan with the water, using the smaller volume if the fruit is ripe and the larger volume plus lemon juice if it is hard.

2 Reserve a few small sprigs of rosemary, then add the rest to the pan. Bring to the boil, reduce the heat, cover with a lid and simmer gently until the fruit becomes pulpy.

3 Remove and discard all the rosemary sprigs. (Don't worry about any tiny leaves that have fallen off during cooking.) Pour the fruit and juices into a sterilized jelly bag suspended over a large bowl. Leave for 3 hours, or until the juices stop dripping.

4 Measure the drained juice into the cleaned pan, adding 450g/1lb/ 2¼ cups sugar for every 600ml/ 1 pint/2½ cups juice.

5 Heat the mixture gently over a low heat, stirring occasionally, until the sugar has dissolved completely. Bring to the boil, then boil rapidly for about 10 minutes until the jelly reaches setting point (105°C/220°F). Remove the pan from the heat.

6 Skim any scum from the surface using a slotted spoon, then leave the jelly to cool for a few minutes until a thin skin begins to form on the surface.

7 Place a sprig of rosemary in each warmed sterilized jar, then pour in the jelly. Cover and seal when cold. Store in a cool, dark place and use within 1 year. Once the jelly is opened, keep it in the refrigerator and use within 3 months.

minted gooseberry jelly

This classic, tart jelly is an ideal complement to roast lamb. Rather surprisingly, the gooseberry juice takes on a pinkish tinge during cooking so does not produce a green jelly as one would expect.

Makes about 1.2kg/2½lb

INGREDIENTS

1.3kg/3lb/12 cups gooseberries
1 bunch fresh mint
750ml/1¼ pints/3 cups cold water
400ml/14fl oz/1⅔ cups white wine vinegar
about 900g/2lb/4½ cups preserving or
 granulated sugar
45ml/3 tbsp chopped fresh mint

1 Place the gooseberries, mint and water in a preserving pan. Bring to the boil, reduce the heat, cover and simmer for about 30 minutes, until the gooseberries are soft. Add the vinegar and simmer uncovered for a further 10 minutes.

2 Pour the fruit and juices into a sterilized jelly bag suspended over a large bowl. Leave to drain for at least 3 hours, or until the juices stop dripping, then measure the strained juices back into the cleaned preserving pan.

3 Add 450g/1lb/2½ cups sugar for every 600ml/1 pint/2½ cups juice, then heat gently, stirring, until the sugar has dissolved. Bring to the boil and cook for 15 minutes, or to setting point (105°C/220°F). Remove the pan from the heat.

4 Skim any scum from the surface. Leave to cool until a thin skin forms, then stir in the mint.

5 Pour the jelly into warmed sterilized jars, cover and seal. Store and use within 1 year. Once opened, store in the refrigerator and eat within 3 months.

plum and apple jelly

Use dark red cooking plums, damsons or wild plums such as bullaces to offset the sweetness of this deep-coloured jelly. Its flavour complements rich roast meats such as lamb and pork.

Makes about 1.3kg/3lb

INGREDIENTS

900g/2lb plums
450g/1lb tart cooking apples
150ml/¼ pint/⅔ cup cider vinegar
750ml/1¼ pints/3 cups water
about 675g/1½lb/scant 3½ cups
 preserving or granulated sugar

COOK'S TIP

This jelly can be stored for up to 2 years. However, once opened, it should be stored in the refrigerator and eaten within 3 months.

1 Cut the plums in half along the crease, twist the two halves apart, then remove the stones (pits) and roughly chop the flesh. Chop the apples, including the cores and skins. Put the fruit in a large heavy pan with the vinegar and water.

2 Bring the mixture to the boil, reduce the heat, cover and simmer for 30 minutes or until the fruit is soft and pulpy.

3 Pour the fruit and juices into a sterilized jelly bag suspended over a large bowl. Leave to drain for at least 3 hours, or until the fruit juices stop dripping.

4 Measure the juice into the cleaned pan, adding 450g/1lb/ 2¼ cups sugar for every 600ml/ 1 pint/2½ cups juice.

5 Bring the mixture to the boil, stirring occasionally, until the sugar has dissolved, then boil rapidly for about 10 minutes, or until the jelly reaches setting point (105°C/220°F). Remove the pan from the heat.

6 Skim any scum from from the surface, then pour the jelly into warmed sterilized jars. Cover and seal while hot. Store in a cool, dark place and use within 2 years.

blackberry and sloe gin jelly

Although they have a wonderful flavour, blackberries are full of pips, so turning them into a deep-coloured jelly is a good way to make the most of this full-flavoured hedgerow harvest. This preserve is delicious served with richly flavoured roast meats such as lamb.

Makes about 1.3kg/3lb

INGREDIENTS

450g/1lb sloes (black plums)
600ml/1 pint/2½ cups cold water
1.8kg/4lb/16 cups blackberries
juice of 1 lemon
about 900g/2lb/4½ cups preserving
  or granulated sugar
45ml/3 tbsp gin

VARIATION

Sloes are much harder to come by than blackberries and you will usually need to find them growing in the wild. If you can't find sloes, use extra blackberries in their place.

1 Wash the sloes and prick with a fine skewer. Put them in a large heavy pan with the water and bring to the boil. Reduce the heat, cover and simmer for 5 minutes.

2 Briefly rinse the blackberries in cold water and add them to the pan with the lemon juice.

3 Bring the fruit mixture back to a simmer and cook gently for about 20 minutes, or until the sloes are tender and the blackberries very soft, stirring once or twice.

4 Pour the fruit and juices into a sterilized jelly bag suspended over a large bowl. Leave to drain for at least 4 hours or overnight, until the juices have stopped dripping.

5 Measure the fruit juice into the cleaned preserving pan, adding 450g/1lb/2¼ cups sugar for every 600ml/1 pint/2½ cups juice.

6 Heat the mixture gently, stirring occasionally, until the sugar has dissolved completely. Bring to the boil, then boil rapidly for about 10 minutes until the jelly reaches setting point (105°C/220°F). Remove the pan from the heat.

7 Skim off any scum from the surface of the jelly using a slotted spoon, then stir in the gin.

8 Pour the jelly into warmed sterilized jars, cover and seal. Store in a cool, dark place and use within 2 years. Once opened, keep the jelly in the refrigerator and eat within 3 months.

COOK'S TIP

Sloes bring a good level of pectin to the jelly. If all blackberries are used without sloes, select some under-ripe fruit and use preserving sugar with added pectin for a good set.

cranberry and claret jelly

The slight sharpness of cranberries makes this a superb jelly for serving with rich meats such as lamb or game. Together with claret, the cranberries give the jelly a beautiful deep red colour.

Makes about 1.2kg/2½lb

INGREDIENTS

900g/2lb/8 cups fresh or
  frozen cranberries
350ml/12fl oz/1½ cups water
about 900g//2lb/4½ cups preserving
  or granulated sugar
250ml/8fl oz/1 cup claret

COOK'S TIP

When simmering the cranberries, keep the pan covered until they stop "popping", as they can occasionally explode and jump out of the pan.

1 Wash the cranberries, if fresh, and put them in a large heavy pan with the water. Cover the pan and bring to the boil.

2 Reduce the heat under the pan and simmer for about 20 minutes, or until the cranberries are soft.

3 Pour the fruit and juices into a sterilized jelly bag suspended over a large bowl. Leave to drain for at least 3 hours or overnight, until the juices stop dripping.

4 Measure the juice and wine into the cleaned preserving pan, adding 400g/14oz/2 cups preserving or granulated sugar for every 600ml/ 1 pint/2½ cups liquid.

5 Heat the mixture gently, stirring occasionally, until the sugar has dissolved, then bring to the boil and boil rapidly for 10 minutes until the jelly reaches setting point (105°C/220°F). Remove the pan from the heat.

6 Skim any scum from the surface using a slotted spoon and pour the jelly into warmed sterilized jars. Cover and seal. Store in a cool, dark place and use within 2 years. Once opened, keep the jelly in the refrigerator and eat within 3 months.

red grape, plum and cardamom jelly

Enhance the flavour of roast beef and steaks with a spoonful of deep ruby-coloured jelly.
You may need to add a little pectin to the jelly to ensure you achieve a really good set.

Makes about 1.3kg/3lb

INGREDIENTS

1.8kg/4lb plums
450g/1lb/3 cups red grapes
15ml/1 tbsp cardamom pods
600ml/1 pint/2½ cups cold water
350–450ml/12fl oz–¾ pint/1½ cups–
   scant 2 cups pectin stock (optional)
about 1kg/2¼lb/5 cups preserving
   or granulated sugar

1 Cut the plums in half, then twist the two halves apart and remove the stone (pit). Roughly chop the flesh and halve the grapes. Remove the cardamom seeds from the pods and crush them in a mortar.

2 Put the fruit and cardamom seeds in a large heavy pan and pour over the water. Slowly bring to the boil, then simmer for about 30 minutes, or until very tender.

3 Check the pectin content of the fruit (see below); if it is low, stir the pectin stock into the fruit mixture and simmer for 5 minutes.

COOK'S TIP

To check the pectin content of the fruit, spoon 5ml/1 tsp of the juices into a glass. Add 15ml/1 tbsp of methylated spirits (denatured alcohol) and shake gently. After about a minute a clot should form. If the clot is large and jelly-like or if two or three smaller clots form, the pectin content should be sufficient for a set. If there are lots of small clots, or none at all, the pectin content is low and additional pectin will be needed.

4 Pour the fruit into a sterilized jelly bag suspended over a large bowl. Leave to drain for 3 hours, or until the juices stop dripping. Measure the juice into a clean pan, adding 450g/1lb/2¼ cups sugar for every 600ml/1 pint/2½ cups juice.

5 Heat the mixture gently, stirring occasionally, until the sugar has completely dissolved.

6 Bring the mixture to the boil, then boil rapidly for 10 minutes until setting point is reached (105°C/220°F). Remove the pan from the heat.

7 Skim off any scum from the surface, then pour the jelly into warmed sterilized jars, cover and seal. Store in a cool, dark place and use within 2 years. Keep in the refrigerator once opened, and eat within 3 months.

pear and pomegranate jelly

This delicate jelly has a faintly exotic perfume. Pears are not naturally rich in pectin so liquid pectin needs to be added to the jelly during cooking to help it achieve a good set.

Makes about 1.2kg/2½lb

INGREDIENTS

900g/2lb pears

pared rind and juice of 2 lemons

1 cinnamon stick

750ml/1¼ pints/3 cups water

900g/2lb red pomegranates

about 900g/2lb/4½ cups preserving or granulated sugar

250ml/8fl oz/1 cup liquid pectin

15ml/1 tbsp rose water (optional)

COOK'S TIP

Once opened, store the jelly in the refrigerator and use within 3 months.

1 Wash and remove the stalks from the pears and chop the fruit roughly. Put the chopped fruit in a large heavy pan with the lemon rind and juice, cinnamon stick and measured water.

2 Bring the mixture to the boil, then reduce the heat to low, cover with a lid and simmer gently for about 15 minutes.

3 Remove the lid from the pan, stir the fruit mixture, then leave to simmer, uncovered, for a further 15 minutes.

4 While the pears are simmering, cut the pomegranates in half horizontally, and use a lemon squeezer to extract all the juice: there should be about 250ml/ 8fl oz/1 cup.

5 Add the pomegranate juice to the pan and bring back to the boil. Reduce the heat and simmer for 2 minutes. Pour the fruit and juices into a sterilized jelly bag suspended over a large bowl. Leave to drip for at least 3 hours.

6 Measure the strained juice into the cleaned pan, adding 450g/1lb/ 2¼ cups sugar for every 600ml/ 1 pint/2½ cups juice.

7 Heat gently, stirring occasionally, until the sugar has dissolved. Bring to the boil, then boil rapidly for 3 minutes. Remove the pan from the heat and stir in the liquid pectin.

8 Skim any scum from the surface, then stir in the rose water, if using. Pour the jelly into warmed sterilized jars. Cover and seal. Store in a cool, dark place and use within 18 months.

guava jelly

Fragrant guava makes an aromatic, pale rust-coloured jelly with a soft set and a slightly sweet-sour flavour that is enhanced by lime juice. Guava jelly goes well with goat's cheese.

Makes about 900g/2lb

INGREDIENTS

900g/2lb guavas
juice of 2–3 limes
about 600ml/1 pint/2½ cups cold water
about 500g/1¼lb/2½ cups preserving
  or granulated sugar

1 Thinly peel and halve the guavas. Using a spoon, scoop out the seeds (pips) from the centre of the fruit and discard them.

2 Place halved guavas in a large heavy pan with 15ml/1 tbsp lime juice and the water – there should be just enough to cover the fruit. Bring the mixture to the boil, then reduce the heat, cover with a lid and simmer for 30 minutes, or until the fruit is tender.

3 Pour the fruit and juices into a sterilized jelly bag suspended over a large bowl. Leave to drain for at least 3 hours.

COOK'S TIP

Do not be tempted to squeeze the jelly bag while the fruit juices are draining from it; this will result in a cloudy jelly.

4 Measure the juice into the cleaned preserving pan, adding 400g/14oz/2 cups sugar and 15ml/1 tbsp lime juice for every 600ml/1 pint/2½ cups guava juice.

5 Heat gently, stirring occasionally, until the sugar has dissolved. Boil rapidly for about 10 minutes. When the jelly reaches setting point, remove the pan from the heat.

6 Skim any scum from the surface of the jelly using a slotted spoon, then pour the jelly into warmed sterilized jars. Cover and seal.

7 Store the jelly in a cool, dark place and use within 1 year. Once opened, keep in the refrigerator and eat within 3 months.

sauces and mustards

No store cupboard is complete without a bottle of tangy sauce and a jar of peppery mustard for serving with hot and cold meats, spreading over cheese on toast, or smearing in a sandwich for an extra spicy bite. Mustard is also indispensable for enlivening mild sauces and dressings – even the smallest spoonful can completely transform a plain cheese sauce or a simple vinaigrette.

sherried plum sauce

Here, plums are cooked with their skins, then strained to make a smooth sauce. Sharp cooking plums, damsons or bullaces give the best flavour and help counteract the sweetness of the sauce, which is wonderful served with roast duck or goose.

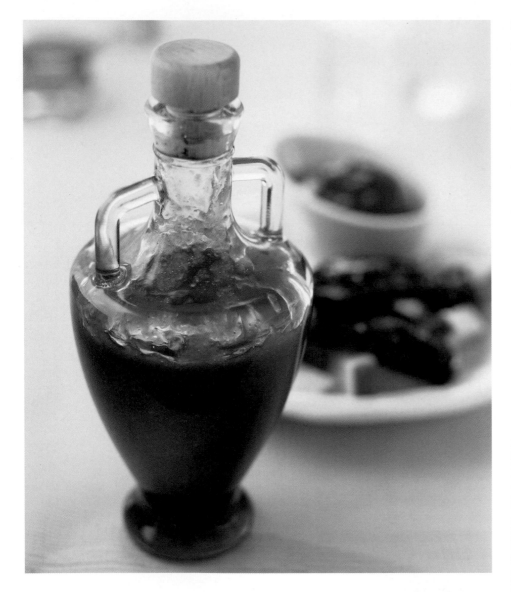

2 Roughly chop the flesh and put in a large, heavy pan. If you're using damsons or bullaces, you may find it easier simply to chop them, leaving in the stones. Stir in the sherry and vinegar.

3 Slowly bring the mixture to the boil, then cover and cook over a gentle heat for about 10 minutes, or until the plums are very soft. Push the fruit through a food mill or sieve to remove the skins.

4 Return the plum purée to the pan and add the sugar, garlic, salt and ginger. Stir until the sugar has dissolved, then bring back to the boil and simmer uncovered for about 15 minutes, until thickened.

Makes about 400ml/14fl oz/1⅔ cups

INGREDIENTS

450g/1lb dark plums or damsons

120ml/4fl oz/½ cup dry sherry, plus extra

30ml/2 tbsp sherry vinegar

175g/6oz/scant 1 cup light muscovado (brown) sugar

1 garlic clove, crushed

1.5ml/¼ tsp salt

2.5cm/1in piece fresh root ginger, finely chopped

3–4 drops of Tabasco sauce

1 Cut each plum in half, then twist apart sand remove the stone (pit).

5 Remove the pan from the heat and stir in the Tabasco sauce. Ladle the sauce into hot sterilized jars. Add 5–10ml/1–2 tsp sherry to the top of each jar, then cover and seal. The sauce will keep for several weeks in the refrigerator or, if heat treated, for 6 months. Once opened, store in the refrigerator and use within 3 weeks.

cumberland sauce

This sauce is thought to have been named after the Duke of Cumberland who became ruler of Hanover at a time when fruit sauces were served with meat and game in Germany. It goes well with cold cuts, pâtés and terrines, and Christmas or Thanksgiving turkey.

Makes about 750ml/1¼ pints/3 cups

INGREDIENTS

4 oranges
2 lemons
450g/1lb redcurrant or rowan jelly
150ml/¼ pint/⅔ cup port
20ml/4 tsp cornflour (cornstarch)
pinch of ground ginger

1 Scrub the oranges and lemons, then remove the rind thinly, paring away any white pith.

2 Cut the orange and lemon rind into very thin matchstick strips. Put the strips in a heavy pan, cover them with cold water and bring the water to the boil.

3 Simmer the rind for 2 minutes, then drain, cover with cold water, bring to the boil and simmer for about 3 minutes. Drain well and return the rind to the pan.

4 Squeeze the juice from the fruits, then add it to the pan with the redcurrant or rowan jelly. Reserve 30ml/2 tbsp of the port and add the rest to the pan.

5 Slowly bring the mixture to the boil, stirring until the jelly has melted. Simmer for 10 minutes until slightly thickened. Blend the cornflour and ginger with the reserved port and stir into the sauce. Cook over a low heat, stirring until the sauce thickens and boils. Simmer for 2 minutes.

6 Leave the sauce to cool for about 5 minutes, then stir again briefly. Pour into warmed sterilized wide-necked bottles or jars, cover and seal. The sauce will keep for several weeks in the refrigerator or, if heat treated, for 6 months. Once opened, store in the refrigerator and use within 3 weeks.

mint sauce

In England, mint sauce is the traditional and inseparable accompaniment to roast lamb. Its fresh, tart, astringent flavour is the perfect foil to rich, strongly flavoured lamb. It is extremely simple to make and is infinitely preferable to the ready-made varieties.

Makes about 250ml/8fl oz/1cup

INGREDIENTS

1 large bunch mint
105ml/7 tbsp boiling water
150ml/¼ pint/⅔ cup wine vinegar
30ml/2 tbsp granulated sugar

COOK'S TIP

To make a quick and speedy Indian raita for serving with crispy poppadums, simply stir a little mint sauce into a small bowl of natural (plain) yogurt. Serve the raita alongside a bowl of tangy mango chutney.

1 Using a sharp knife, chop the mint very finely and place it in a 600ml/1 pint/2½ cup jug (pitcher). Pour the boiling water over the mint and leave to infuse for about 10 minutes.

2 When the mint infusion has cooled and is lukewarm, stir in the wine vinegar and sugar. Continue stirring (but do not mash up the mint leaves) until the sugar has dissolved completely.

3 Pour the mint sauce into a sterilized bottle or jar, seal and store in the refrigerator.

COOK'S TIP

This mint sauce can keep for up to 6 months stored in the refrigerator, but is best used within 3 weeks.

traditional horseradish sauce

Fiery, peppery horseradish sauce is without doubt the essential accompaniment to roast beef and is also delicious served with smoked salmon. Horseradish, like chillies, is a powerful ingredient so you should take care when handling it and wash your hands straight afterwards.

Makes about 200ml/7fl oz/scant 1 cup

INGREDIENTS

45ml/3 tbsp freshly grated
  horseradish root
15ml/1 tbsp white wine vinegar
5ml/1 tsp granulated sugar
pinch of salt
150ml/¼ pint/⅔ cup thick double
  (heavy) cream, for serving

COOK'S TIP

To counteract the potent fumes of the horseradish, keep the root submerged in water while you chop and peel it. Use a food procssor to do the fine chopping or grating, and avert your head when removing the lid.

1 Place the grated horseradish in a bowl, then add the white wine vinegar, granulated sugar and just a pinch of salt.

2 Stir the ingredients together until thoroughly combined.

3 Pour the mixture into a sterilized jar. It will keep in the refrigerator for up to 6 months.

4 A few hours before you intend to serve the sauce, stir the cream into the horseradish and leave to infuse.

tangy tomato ketchup

Sweet, tangy, spicy tomato ketchup is perfect for serving with barbecued or grilled burgers and sausages. This home-made variety is so much better than store-bought tomato ketchup.

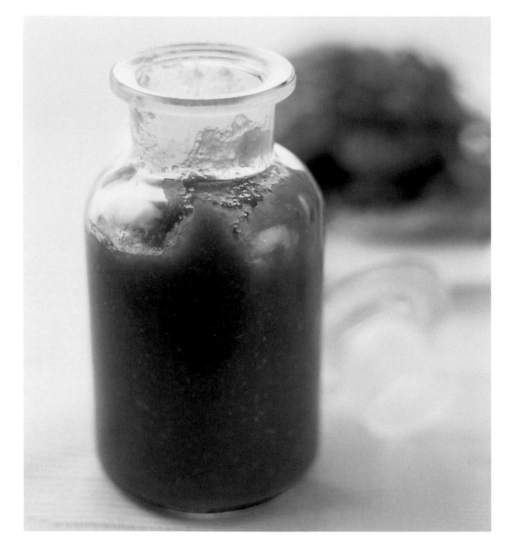

2 Tie the onion with the allspice, peppercorns, rosemary and ginger into a double layer of muslin (cheesecloth) and add to the pan. Chop the celery, plus the leaves, and add to the pan with the sugar, raspberry vinegar, garlic and salt.

3 Bring the mixture to the boil over a fairly high heat, stirring occasionally. Reduce the heat and simmer for 1½–2 hours, stirring regularly, until reduced by half. Purée the mixture in a food processor, then return to the pan, bring to the boil and simmer for 15 minutes. Bottle in clean, sterilized jars and store in the refrigerator. Use within 2 weeks.

Makes about 1.3kg/3lb

INGREDIENTS

2.25kg/5lb very ripe tomatoes

1 onion

6 cloves

4 allspice berries

6 black peppercorns

1 fresh rosemary sprig

25g/1oz fresh root ginger, sliced

1 celery heart

30ml/2 tbsp soft light brown sugar

65ml/4½ tbsp raspberry vinegar

3 garlic cloves, peeled

15ml/1 tbsp salt

1 Carefully peel and seed the ripe tomatoes, then chop and place in a large pan. Peel the onion, leaving the tip and root intact and stud it with the cloves.

barbecue sauce

As well as enlivening burgers and other food cooked on the barbecue, this sauce is also good for all manner of grilled meats and savoury pastries.

Makes about 900ml/1½ pints/3¾ cups

INGREDIENTS

30ml/2 tbsp olive oil

1 large onion, chopped

1 garlic clove, crushed

1 fresh red chilli, seeded and sliced

2 celery sticks, sliced

1 large carrot, sliced

1 medium cooking apple, quartered, cored, peeled and chopped

450g/1lb ripe tomatoes, quartered

2.5ml/½ tsp ground ginger

150ml/¼ pint/⅔ cup malt vinegar

1 bay leaf

4 whole cloves

4 black peppercorns

50g/2oz/¼ cup soft light brown sugar

10ml/2 tsp English mustard

2.5ml/½ tsp salt

1 Heat the oil in a large heavy pan. Add the onion and cook over a low heat for 5 minutes.

2 Stir in the garlic, chilli, celery and carrot into the onions and cook for 5 minutes, stirring frequently, until the onion just begins to colour.

3 Add the apple, tomatoes, ground ginger and malt vinegar to the pan and stir to combine.

4 Put the bay leaf, cloves and peppercorns on a square of muslin (cheesecloth) and tie into a bag with fine string. Add to the pan and bring to the boil. Reduce the heat, cover and simmer for about 45 minutes, stirring occasionally.

5 Add the sugar, mustard and salt to the pan and stir until the sugar dissolves. Simmer for 5 minutes. Leave to cool for 10 minutes, then remove the bag and discard.

6 Press the mixture through a sieve and return to the cleaned pan. Simmer for 10 minutes, or until thickened. Adjust the seasoning.

7 Pour the sauce into hot sterilized bottles or jars, then seal. Heat process, cool and, if using cork-topped bottles, dip the corks in wax. Store in a cool, dark place and use within 1 year. Once opened, store in the refrigerator and use within 2 months.

roasted red pepper and chilli ketchup

Roasting the peppers gives this ketchup a richer, smoky flavour. You can add fewer or more chillies according to taste. Once opened, store in the refrigerator and use within 3 months.

Makes about 600ml/1 pint/2½ cups

INGREDIENTS

900g/2lb red (bell) peppers

225g/8oz shallots

1 tart cooking apple, quartered, cored and roughly chopped

4 fresh red chillies, seeded and chopped

1 large sprig each thyme and parsley

1 bay leaf

5ml/1 tsp coriander seeds

5ml/1 tsp black peppercorns

600ml/1 pint/2½ cups water

350ml/12fl oz/1½ cups red wine vinegar

50g/2oz/scant ¼ cup granulated sugar

5ml/1 tsp salt

7.5ml/1½ tsp arrowroot

1 Preheat the grill (broiler). Place the peppers on a baking sheet and grill for 10–12 minutes, turning regularly, until the skins have blackened. Put the peppers in a plastic bag and leave for 5 minutes.

2 When the peppers are cool enough to handle, peel away the skin, then quarter the peppers and remove the seeds. Roughly chop the flesh and place in a large pan.

3 Put the shallots in a bowl, pour over boiling water and leave to stand for 3 minutes. Drain, then rinse under cold water and peel. Chop the shallots and add to the pan with the apple and chillies.

4 Tie the thyme, parsley, bay leaf, coriander and peppercorns together in a square of muslin (cheesecloth).

5 Add the bag of herbs and the water to the pan and bring to the boil. Reduce the heat, cover and simmer for 30 minutes. Leave to cool for 15 minutes, then remove and discard the muslin bag.

6 Purée the mixture in a food processor, then press through a sieve and return the purée to the cleaned pan. Reserve 15ml/1 tbsp of the vinegar and add the rest to the pan with the sugar and salt.

7 Bring to the boil, stirring until the sugar has dissolved, then simmer for 45 minutes, or until the sauce is well reduced. Blend the arrowroot with the reserved vinegar, stir into the sauce, then simmer for a 2–3 minutes, or until slightly thickened.

8 Pour the sauce into hot sterilized bottles, then seal, heat process and store in a cool, dark place and use within 18 months.

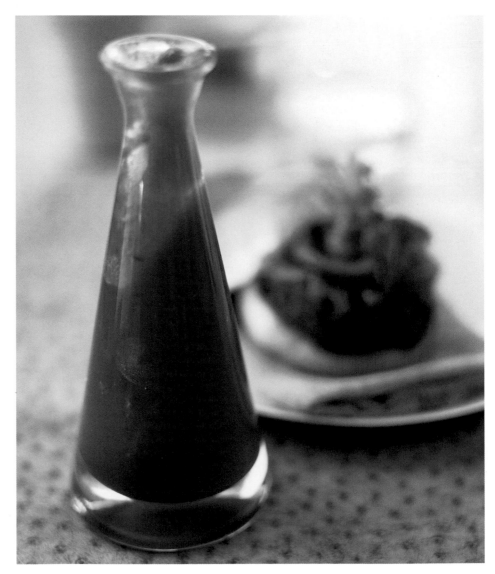

aromatic mustard powder

This pungent condiment has the added flavour of herbs and spices and should be served in small quantities with meats and cheese. To serve, simply mix it with a little water.

Makes about 200g/7oz/1⅔ cups

INGREDIENTS

115g/4oz/1 cup mustard powder
25ml/1½ tbsp ground sea salt
5ml/1 tsp dried thyme
5ml/1 tsp dried tarragon
5ml/1 tsp mixed spice (apple
  pie spice)
2.5ml/½ tsp ground black pepper
2.5ml/½ tsp garlic powder (optional)

1 Put the mustard powder and salt in a small bowl and stir together until evenly blended.

2 Add the dried thyme and tarragon to the mustard with the mixed spice, ground black pepper and garlic powder, if using. Stir until thoroughly mixed.

3 Spoon the mustard powder into small clean, dry jars, then seal tightly. Store it in a cool, dark place and use within 6 months. (Although the mustard powder won't go off, the potency of the herbs and spices will fade with age and the final mustard will not have the same lovely, strong flavour.)

4 To serve, combine the mustard powder with an equal amount of cold water 10 minutes before needed. Mix well until smooth.

COOK'S TIPS

• The mustard is best when freshly made, so mix up small quantities as and when you need it.

• To sharpen the flavour when serving the mustard with rich meats, use about a third cider or tarragon vinegar and two-thirds water. It can also be blended with sherry, white or red wine or port; the latter two will give the mustard a darker colour.

• The mustard powder is also great added to sauces and salad dressings to give extra flavour.

moutarde aux fines herbes

This classic, fragrant mustard may be used either as a delicious condiment or for coating meats such as chicken and pork, or oily fish such as mackerel, before cooking. It is also fabulous smeared thinly on cheese on toast for an added bite.

Makes about 300ml/½ pint/1¼ cups

INGREDIENTS

75g/3oz/scant ½ cup white mustard seeds

50g/2oz/¼ cup soft light brown sugar

5ml/1 tsp salt

5ml/1 tsp whole peppercorns

2.5ml/½ tsp ground turmeric

200ml/7fl oz/scant 1 cup distilled malt vinegar

60ml/4 tbsp chopped fresh mixed herbs, such as parsley, sage, thyme and rosemary

COOK'S TIP

Stir a spoonful of this fragrant mustard into creamy savoury sauces and salad dressings to enhance their flavour.

1 Put the mustard seeds, sugar, salt, whole peppercorns and ground turmeric into a food processor or blender and process for about 1 minute, or until the peppercorns are coarsely chopped.

2 Gradually add the vinegar to the mustard mixture, 15ml/1 tbsp at a time, processing well between each addition, then continue processing until a coarse paste forms.

3 Add the chopped fresh herbs to the mustard and mix well, then leave to stand for 10–15 minutes until the mustard thickens slightly.

4 Spoon the mustard into a 300ml/ ½ pint/1¼ cup sterilized jar. Cover the surface of the mustard with a greaseproof (waxed) paper disc, then seal with a screw-top lid or a cork, and label. Store in a cool, dark place.

honey mustard

Delicious home-made mustards mature to make the most aromatic of condiments. This honey mustard is richly flavoured and is wonderful served with meats and cheeses or stirred into sauces and salad dressings to give an extra, peppery bite. The addition of honey gives the mustard a deliciously rounded, full, slightly sweet flavour.

Makes about 500g/1¼lb

INGREDIENTS

225g/8oz/1 cup mustard seeds

15ml/1 tbsp ground cinnamon

2.5ml/½ tsp ground ginger

300ml/½ pint/1¼ cups white wine vinegar

90ml/6 tbsp dark clear honey

COOK'S TIP

Make sure you use well-flavoured clear, runny honey for this recipe. Set (crystallized) honey does not have the right consistency and will not work well.

1 Put the mustard seeds in a bowl with the spices and pour over the vinegar. Stir well to mix, then leave to soak overnight.

2 The next day, put the mustard mixture in a mortar and pound with a pestle, adding the honey very gradually.

3 Continue pounding and mixing until the mustard resembles a stiff paste. If the mixture is too stiff, add a little extra vinegar to achieve the desired consistency.

4 Spoon the mustard into four sterilized jars, seal and label, then store in the refrigerator and use within 4 weeks.

COOK'S TIP

This sweet, spicy mustard is perfect for adding extra flavour to cheese tarts or quiches. Spread a very thin layer of mustard across the base of the pastry case before adding the filling, then bake according to the recipe. The mustard will really complement the cheese, giving a mouth-watering result.

tarragon and champagne mustard

This delicately flavoured mustard is well worth making and goes particularly well with cold chicken, fish and shellfish. Its mild taste enhances these foods perfectly.

Makes about 250g/9oz

INGREDIENTS

30ml/2 tbsp mustard seeds

75ml/5 tbsp champagne vinegar

115g/4oz/1 cup mustard powder

115g/4oz/½ cup soft light brown sugar

2.5ml/½ tsp salt

50ml/3½ tbsp virgin olive oil

60ml/4 tbsp chopped fresh tarragon

COOK'S TIP

Champagne vinegar has a lovely flavour but can sometimes be hard to find. Look in specialist delicatessens and food stores, or large supermarkets that stock a good range of gourmet foods.

1 Put the mustard seeds and vinegar in a bowl and leave to soak overnight.

2 The next day, tip the mustard seeds and vinegar into a food processor and add the mustard powder, sugar and salt.

3 Blend the mustard mixture until smooth, then slowly add the oil while continuing to blend.

4 Tip the mustard into a bowl, stir in the tarragon, then spoon into sterilized jars, seal and store in a cool, dark place.

horseradish mustard

This tangy mustard has a wonderfully creamy, peppery taste and is an excellent accompaniment to cold meats, smoked fish or cheese. It is also effective spread thinly inside cold roast beef sandwiches – a great alternative to the traditional horseradish sauce.

Makes about 400g/14oz

INGREDIENTS

25ml/1½ tbsp mustard seeds

250ml/8fl oz/1 cup boiling water

115g/4oz/1 cup mustard powder

115g/4oz/scant ½ cup granulated sugar

120ml/4fl oz/½ cup white wine
  or cider vinegar

50ml/2fl oz/¼ cup olive oil

5ml/1 tsp lemon juice

30ml/2 tbsp horseradish sauce

COOK'S TIP

For the best results, use home-made horseradish sauce.

1 Put the mustard seeds in a bowl and pour over the boiling water. Set aside and leave to soak for at least 1 hour.

2 Drain the mustard seeds and discard the soaking liquid, then tip the seeds into a food processor or blender.

3 Add the mustard powder, sugar, white wine or cider vinegar, olive oil, lemon juice and horseradish sauce to the mustard seeds in the food processor or blender.

4 Process the ingredients into a smooth paste, then spoon the mustard into sterilized jars. Store the mustard in the refrigerator and use within 3 months.

spiced tamarind mustard

Tamarind has a distinctive sweet and sour flavour, a dark brown colour and sticky texture. Combined with spices and ground mustard seeds, it makes a wonderful condiment.

Makes about 200g/7oz

INGREDIENTS

115g/4oz tamarind block

150ml/¼ pint/⅔ cup warm water

50g/2oz/¼ cup yellow mustard seeds

25ml/1½ tbsp black or brown
  mustard seeds

10ml/2 tsp clear honey

pinch of ground cardamom

pinch of salt

COOK'S TIP

The mustard will be ready to eat in 3–4 days. It should be stored in a cool, dark place and used within 4 months.

1 Put the tamarind in a small bowl and pour over the water. Leave to soak for 30 minutes. Mash to a pulp with a fork, then strain through a fine sieve into a bowl.

2 Grind the mustard seeds in a spice mill or coffee grinder and add to the tamarind with the remaining ingredients. Spoon into sterilized jars, cover and seal.

clove-spiced mustard

This spicy mustard is the perfect accompaniment to robust red meats such as sausages and steaks, particularly when they are cooked on the barbecue.

Makes about 300ml/½ pint/1¼ cups

INGREDIENTS

75g/3oz/scant ½ cup white
  mustard seeds

50g/2oz/¼ cup soft light brown sugar

5ml/1 tsp salt

5ml/1 tsp black peppercorns

5ml/1 tsp cloves

5ml/1 tsp turmeric

200ml/7fl oz/scant 1 cup distilled
  malt vinegar

COOK'S TIP

Cloves add a lovely, warming taste to this mustard. Make sure you use whole cloves in this mustard – ground cloves tend to have less flavour.

1 Put all the ingredients except the malt vinegar into a food processor or blender and process. Gradually add the vinegar, 15ml/1 tbsp at a time, processing well between each addition. Continue processing the mustard until it forms a fairly thick, coarse paste.

2 Leave the mustard to stand for 10–15 minutes to thicken slightly. Spoon into a 300ml/½ pint/1¼ cup sterilized jar or several smaller jars, using a funnel. Cover the surface with a greaseproof (waxed) paper disc, then seal with a screw-top lid or a cork, and label.

INDEX